MAMA MAKES
UP HER MIND

Bailey White teaches first grade in South Georgia, where she lives with her mother. Her essays and stories have appeared in several magazines.

Bailey White

MAMA MAKES UP HER MIND

and Other Dangers of Southern Living

V

VINTAGE

Published by Vintage 1995

2 4 6 8 10 9 7 5 3

First published in the United States of America by
Addison-Wesley, 1993

Portions of this book have appeared in different form
in *Smithsonian*, *Tropic*, *Northeast* and other magazines,
and have been heard on National Public Radio's
All Things Considered.

Vintage
Random House, 20 Vauxhall Bridge Road, London SW1V 2SA

Random House Australia (Pty) Limited
20 Alfred Street, Milsons Point, Sydney
New South Wales 2061, Australia

Random House New Zealand Limited
18 Poland Road, Glenfield,
Auckland 10, New Zealand

Random House South Africa (Pty) Limited
PO Box 337, Bergvlei, South Africa

Random House UK Limited Reg. No. 954009

A CIP catalogue record for this book
is available from the British Library

ISBN 0 09 945041 0

Printed and bound in Great Britain by
The Guernsey Press Co. Ltd., Guernsey, Channel Islands

Contents

Contents

Contents

Acknowledgments

I would like to thank Daniel Pinkwater and Margaret Low Smith, and all my kind friends at National Public Radio, for their support and encouragement.

Mama Makes Up Her Mind

Rosey's

The other day Mama made up her mind she wanted some smoked mullet.

"Does this mean we have to go down to Rosey's?" I asked.

"Yep," she said.

Rosey's is a tough juke joint on the edge of the marsh in an old-fashioned part of Florida. Tourists don't go there; they've got more sense. At Rosey's you never know whether you're drunk or not because the floors wave up and down anyway. The foundations are sagging. You can eat inside if you can take the smoke, or you can eat outside and throw your fish bones down to some rough-looking pelicans who squat like vultures under the porch. Ernest Hemingway went there once, but the atmosphere was too much for him.

I don't like to go to Rosey's. I'm always afraid some of those people shooting pool in the back will think I'm the one who chose that goofy song that's playing on the jukebox, put down their pool cues, and beat me up. But Mama doesn't notice. She just likes the smoked mullet.

We sat inside. I was afraid Mama might lose her balance on the porch, tip off the edge, and get eaten up by the pelicans. I crept up to the counter to order. I kept my head down and tried not to swing my arms. "One order of smoked mullet, and one unsweet iced tea, please," I said. Rosey flung the mullet onto a plate, then lifted the scum off the top of the tea with one finger and flicked it on the floor. "Don't get much orders for iced tea," she said.

Mama ate her mullet and I drank my tea. Pretty soon I had to go to the bathroom. There was a sign that said Restrooms over two doors. One of the doors said Men, and the other one said Men. I didn't like to ask. "I'll ask," said Mama. And she headed up to the counter.

When Mama starts to move across a room, people pay attention. You can never be sure she's not going to grab you by the top of the head to steady herself. And she's pretty free with that walking stick, too. The room grew quiet. I don't know whether it was the faltering gait or the look in her eye or the mismatched safety pins holding her glasses together or the Band-Aid with the "Sesame Street" characters on it on her arm, but by the time she got to the counter, everybody was watching.

"Where's the bathroom?" she said. "The women's bathroom." She paused. "My daughter," she pointed with her walking stick, "my daughter wants to know."

Spyglass

My father craved an adventurous life, and when I was just a little girl, he went off with an anthropological team from the Field Museum of Natural History to study and record the physical characteristics of four fierce groups of people in southwestern Asia. My father had no training as an anthropometrist, and his job on the expedition, as close as we could figure it, was to grab the subjects and hold them still while the scientists applied the spreading calipers and the anthropometer, and took hair and blood samples "where possible."

The leader of the expedition, a famous physical anthropologist, was a kind gentleman, and he took pity on my mother, who was to be left at home for a year and a half with a farm to run and three unruly children, and he gave her, as a parting gift, his telescope. It was a beautiful instrument, all gleaming brass and leather and ebony, with a wonderfully silent sliding action and a muffled *thunk* as it achieved its full-open position. On the day they left, Professor Meade laid it in my mother's hands. "My great-grandfather had it at Trafalgar," he told her. "Now I want you to have it." Then he said good-bye and swept away, leaving us in a swirl of English pipe tobacco, old leather, and oiled canvas, my father staggering along behind him, dragging the cases of clattering instruments.

The year and a half went by, and my mother studied every distant object she could find, from celestial bodies in the night sky to the pond a mile away from our house, which through the lenses of · Professor Meade's telescope looked like a bright, magical place where frogs leapt silently and deer drinking at the water's edge had no fear of people.

My father came back, sunburned and irritable. He had presents for us: for my brother, a Persian dagger with a jeweled handle; for my mother, a lamp made out of the bladders of two camels; and for my sister and me, exquisite rag dolls that had little hands with separated fingers like real hands, and ferocious embroidered faces with furious dark eyes and sullen red satin-stitched lips.

My brother developed amazing skills with the dagger and terrorized the neighborhood with feats of knife throwing, and my mother, on a creative whim, turned the camel-bladder lamp upside down and hung it by an electrical cord over the dining-room table. She wouldn't let us play with the dolls. She suspected lice and packed them away in moth-balls. My father himself had a serious infestation of crabs—some virulent southwestern Asian strain impervious to the pediculicides of the New World.

Soon my father went off on another adventure, but this time he never came back. The camel-bladder chandelier could not seem to adjust to the climate of south Georgia: in the summer it would droop and swag and stretch in the damp heat until it almost touched the tabletop, and in the winter it would shrink and suck itself into a tight snarl up near the ceiling.

The years went by. My mother got old and crip-pled. And as her mobility decreased, she grew more and more dependent on Professor Meade's tele-scope. "Bring me my spyglass!" she would call. Someone would fetch it, she would put her elbows on the windowsill, lean the shaft of the telescope against the frame, and gaze.

Then one day we got a telephone call from a granddaughter of Professor Meade's. She wanted to see us "on a matter of some importance," she said. She flew down from Chicago. Professor Meade was on his deathbed. He was dying peacefully. There was only one thing he wanted: his grandfather's telescope.

My brother was incensed. He had recently taken the telescope apart into its thousand pieces to clean the lenses and change the felts. It had taken him two weeks. "What does a dying man need with a telescope?" he fumed.

My sister and I asked, "Now what will Mama look at things through?"

But it didn't bother Mama one bit. "His great-grandfather had it at Trafalgar," she said. "Of course he shall have it back." And she carefully slid the telescope into its Morocco leather case, snapped the snaps, and gave it to Professor Meade's granddaughter.

And Mama didn't seem to miss it. As a premium in the thirty-dollar pledge category for the local public radio station she got a pair of tiny plastic binoculars. Looking through those binoculars was the equivalent of taking three steps closer to your subject. "But it's hard for me to take three steps," she pointed out, the binoculars clamped to her eyes. She used to be able to sweep the telescope into position, with the near distance, middle distance, and remote distance swirling and colliding in brilliant, sharp disarray, and then focus on an osprey catching a fish a mile away, a silent explosion of bright water. Now, with the binoculars, she could see the purple finches on the bird feeder at the kitchen window a bit clearer, and recognize friends and family members when they came to call

9

a moment before they opened the screen door, stepped inside, and said to her, "Put those damned binoculars down, Lila."

One summer we made a family trek to a wild island off the coast of north Florida. We stayed in a house with a big screen porch on the bay side. It was hard for Mama to walk on the soft sand, so she sat on the porch all day, staring through her binoculars out over the marsh.

Every morning a boat from the local marine lab would pull up and anchor just off shore. People would wade around in the marsh grass with nets and spades and bottles. By the end of the first week the screen was bulged out from the pressure of Mama's binoculars. She didn't seem to understand that they did not give her the same dignity of distance she had been able to achieve with the telescope. We tried to reason with her. "They can see you, Mama," we hissed. But she just pressed the binoculars harder against the screen.

"What are they doing? What are they doing down there?" she asked.

Then one evening a man came up to the house. We recognized him from the morning marine lab group. "Oh no," we thought.

"Where is that old woman with the little tiny binoculars?" he asked. We shuffled around and shuffled around. Someone went and got her from in the house.

He shook her hand. "My name is Lewis," he said,

"Walter Lewis. Would you like to see what we're doing down there?" And very carefully he helped her over the sand to the marsh.

For the rest of our stay on the island, Mama would make her way down the beach every morning. She would sit in a chair at the water's edge and look at the things they brought up.

"It's clams," she told us. "They're studying a certain kind of clam." Dr. Lewis gave her books, and she sat up all night reading about bivalve mollusks.

At the end of our last week on the island Dr. Lewis came up to the house to say good-bye. "A group of us from the marine lab are leaving this afternoon to do a little more work on the migration of the spiny lobster," he said to Mama. "We thought you might like to come along."

The last we saw of Mama that summer, she was heading for the open ocean. We stood on the dock and waved good-bye. But she didn't see us. She was leaning forward in the bow of the boat with her little plastic binoculars pressed to her eyes, peering out to sea.

Turkeys

Something about my mother attracts ornithologists. It all started years ago when a couple of them discovered she had a rare species of woodpecker coming to her bird feeder. They came in the house and sat around the window, exclaiming and taking pictures with big fancy cameras. But long after the red cockaded woodpeckers had gone to roost in their sticky little holes in the red hearts of our big old pine trees, and the chuck-will's-widows had started to sing their night chorus, the ornithologists were still there. There always seemed to be three or four of them wandering around our place, discussing the body fat of hummingbirds, telling cruel jokes about people who couldn't tell a pileated woodpecker from an ivory bill, and staying for supper.

In those days, during the 1950s, the big concern of ornithologists in our area was the wild turkey. They were rare, and the pure-strain wild turkeys had begun to interbreed with farmers' domestic stock. The species was being degraded. It was extinction by dilution, and to the ornithologists it was just as tragic as the more dramatic demise of the passenger pigeon or the Carolina parakeet.

One ornithologist had devised a formula to compute the ratio of domestic to pure-strain wild turkey in an individual bird by comparing the angle of flight at takeoff and the rate of acceleration. And in those sad days, the turkeys were flying low and slow.

It was during that time, the spring when I was six years old, that I caught the measles. I had a high fever, and my mother was worried about me. She kept the house quiet and dark and crept around silently, trying different methods of cooling me down.

Even the ornithologists stayed away—but not out of fear of the measles or respect for a household with sickness. The fact was, they had discovered a wild turkey nest. According to the formula, the hen was pure-strain wild—not a taint of the sluggish domestic bird in her blood—and the ornithologists were camping in the woods, protecting her nest from predators and taking pictures.

One night our phone rang. It was one of the ornithologists. "Does your little girl still have measles?" he asked.

"Yes," said my mother. "She's very sick. Her temperature is 102."

"I'll be right over," said the ornithologist.

In five minutes a whole carload of them arrived. They marched solemnly into the house, carrying a cardboard box. "A hundred two, did you say? Where is she?" they asked my mother.

They crept into my room and set the box down on the bed. I was barely conscious, and when I opened my eyes, their worried faces hovering over me seemed to float out of the darkness like giant, glowing eggs. They snatched the covers off me and felt me all over. They consulted in whispers.

"Feels just right, I'd say."

"A hundred two—can't miss if we tuck them up close and she lies still."

I closed my eyes then, and after a while the ornithologists drifted away, their pale faces bobbing up and down on the black wave of fever.

The next morning I was better. For the first time in days I could think. The memory of the ornithologists with their whispered voices and their bony, cool hands was like a dream from another life. But when I pulled down the covers, there staring up at me with googly eyes and wide mouths, were sixteen fuzzy baby turkeys and the cracked chips and caps of sixteen brown speckled eggs.

I was a sensible child. I gently stretched myself out. The eggshells crackled, and the turkey babies fluttered and cheeped and snuggled against me. I laid my aching head back on the pillow and closed my eyes. "The ornithologists," I whispered. "The ornithologists have been here."

It seems the turkey hen had been so disturbed by the elaborate protective measures that had been undertaken in her behalf that she had abandoned her nest on the night the eggs were due to hatch. It was a cold night. The ornithologists, not having an incubator to hand, used their heads and came up with the next best thing.

The baby turkeys and I gained our strength together. When I was finally able to get out of bed and feebly creep around the house, the turkeys peeped and cheeped around my ankles, scrambling to keep up with me and tripping over their own big spraddle-toed feet. When I went outside for the first time, the turkeys tumbled after me down the steps and scratched around in the yard while I sat in the sun.

Finally, in late summer, the day came when they were ready to fly for the first time as adult birds. The ornithologists gathered. I ran down the hill, and the turkeys ran too. Then, one by one, they took off. They flew high and fast. The ornithologists made V's with their thumbs and forefingers, measuring angles. They consulted their stopwatches and paced off distances. They scribbled in their tiny notebooks. Finally they looked at each other. They sighed. They smiled. They jumped up and down and hugged each other. "One hundred percent pure wild turkey!" they said.

Nearly forty years have passed since then. In many ways the world is a worse place now. But there's a vaccine for measles. And the woods where I live are full of pure wild turkeys. I like to think they are all descendants of those sixteen birds I saved from the vigilance of the ornithologists.

Midnight Cowboy

Every so often I take my mother to the movies. She has quite definite opinions and tastes, so I always have to see the movie first. If I think it would suit her, we go back to the Sunday matinee.

Her favorite of all time is *Midnight Cowboy*. It is the standard by which all movies must be judged. She has seen *King of Hearts*, *Annie Hall*, and *Babette's Feast*. When she comes out of the theater, she'll consider a while. "Well," I'll say, "what did you think?" She always shakes her head and says, "It was good, but it's no *Midnight Cowboy*."

My mother is old and feeble. She should use one of those four-legged aluminum walkers, but instead she teeters around precariously on her tiny little feet. She has a walking stick, but she hasn't got the knack of it yet. She waves it around and pokes things with it. When we go to the movies, I have to help her get over the curb, set her down in the lobby, and go park the car. Then I buy the tickets and we go in.

Last week I took her to see *Presumed Innocent*. I got her into the theater and went to park the car. When I came back, there she was drinking Coca-Cola from a quart-sized cup and balancing a gallon of popcorn on her knee. There was a crowd of teenagers standing around her. They were staring at her and eating Raisinettes. She was telling them the story of *Midnight Cowboy*. She was acting out her favorite parts.

"Now," she said, "this movie, *Presumed Innocent*—is it as good as that?"

"Jeez, no," they said, "it's good, but it's not that good."

Porsche

Mama and I live in one of those houses where things accumulate. Something can get laid down on a table or in the seat of a broken chair and just stay there forever. There's my great-grandmother's coat she hung on a nail before she died, and an old cousin's unfinished model of the *Flying Cloud*. There's a couple of bamboo chinaberry-seed popguns from three generations back and six bottles of Maybloom Cream beginning to turn iridescent with the tops rusted on. There's a row of Mason jars with some spooky-looking mold growing inside, left over from an old dead aunt's experiments with lethal herbs, and a drop-seat viyella union suit folded up on top of the carburetor of a Model A Ford. After a while the things begin to interlock. I really don't think we could get the ship model out in one piece even if we tried.

When I was eight years old, it got to be too much for my father. I remember the day he left for good. "I can't take it anymore!" he wailed. "I'm stagnating here! That coat!" He clutched the top of his head. I looked at my great-grandmother's coat. "That coat has been hanging there for fifty years!" And he hurled himself out of the house, jumped into his little red Porsche, and scratched off in a swirl of dust.

I missed my father. "Why don't we move the coat?" I asked my mother. "Then maybe he'll come back."

"It's not just the coat, child," she told me. I looked around. There were my great-aunt Bertie's lavender satin wedding shoes perched on the seat of my Uncle Luten's unicycle, and Uncle Ralph's wall-eyed, hunchbacked, one-legged stuffed turkey on the library table. She was right. Even I could see it wasn't just the coat.

We never saw my father again, but we heard that he had driven that Porsche all the way to Hollywood, California, and made piles of money writing scripts for TV shows. Our neighbors told us they had actually seen his name on TV. We wouldn't know. We didn't have a TV set. Where would we have put it?

The years went by. Twenty years, thirty years. Then one fall my father died. His fourth wife, now his widow, called us on the phone. "He left you something," she said. "It should be there in a few days."

And a week later it arrived. It was my father's Porsche, the same one he had left us in—a 1958 Model 356 speedster, in original condition, complete with a wild-eyed driver whose hair stood straight up on end. Mama told him, "Just park it out behind the garden with those two tractors and that thing that might have been a lawnmower."

But he wouldn't do it. "Lady, you're crazy. You don't know what this is." He rubbed the car's fender with his shirttail. "You don't park a car like this out with the tractors."

We stood around and looked at it. Mama sighed. Then she went over and started pulling a section of screen off the side porch. We built a ramp, and the man drove the car up onto the porch. We drained the oil and gas out of it, put it up on blocks, and replaced the screen.

Now a man who says he belongs to the Porsche Club of America calls us up almost every night hoping to buy the car. We keep telling him no, no, no. Besides, that car has been in our house almost a year now. Even if he came all the way down here, I doubt he could get to it.

Instant Care

Mama wasn't feeling too good. She had a little fever, and she said her bones ached. I talked her into going to her doctor. Dr. Perkins is as old as she is, and he was not in his office. He was sick, too.

The nurse suggested we go out to the new Instant Care Facility at the shopping center. It's out there between the grocery store and the ten-minute oil change and lube station. You just walk in and within minutes a teenaged nurse weighs you, measures you, takes your blood pressure, pricks your finger, gets you into a tissue-paper gown, and sets you up on the padded table still warm from the last wretched soul. Then a generic doctor bustles in and prescribes medicine, which you can pick up at Quick Drugs across the street.

I let Mama out at the curb and pointed her to the entrance of the Instant Care Facility. Then I parked the car and went to do some grocery shopping. When I came out, there she was, standing on the sidewalk talking to three butchers from the grocery store who were taking a cigarette break.

"That didn't take long," I said.

"No," she said, "and such very nice young doctors."

I was surprised. She hadn't been too keen on Instant Care when Dr. Perkins's nurse had suggested it. "I just know it will be all those flashes of light where no light ought to be, and invisible probes nosing into Lord-knows-where," she had complained.

But no, she said now, they had been very patient, had listened to her describe her symptoms, and had told her to pick up some Thomas's Cold Tablets at the old drugstore downtown. "Quick Drugs doesn't carry them," Mama said.

We went downtown for the medicine, then home. Mama took two of the Thomas's Cold Tablets and went to bed. The next day she was well.

"I highly recommend that Instant Care Facility," she said. "And do you know, I didn't even have to get undressed? Why, I didn't even have to go inside!"

"What?" I said.

"Sidewalk diagnosis," she declared. "And free! Didn't cost me a dime. And three doctors all at once."

"Wait a minute," I said, "you mean those three men I saw you talking to outside Safeway? You mean those three men smoking Lucky Strike cigarettes in those white coats with blood smeared all around the pockets? Those were your doctors?"

"Yes," she said, "vigorous doctors—the old-fashioned kind. Surgeons, I'd say, from the amount of blood and brains on those white coats."

Bicyclists

It was one of those accidents of remodeling. Everyone knows the kind of thing: you hang a door in your new bathroom, and then when you go to close it for the first time, it bangs into the sink. Ours was worse, though. We ended up, when the carpenter had swept up and driven off with his tools, with a bathtub on a screen porch. It's one of those high-sided tubs with claw feet, piped for hot and cold. We puzzled over it for a few days; then we just gave up, bought a soap dish, and hung a towel on a nail. The tub drains out into a bed of semiaquatic lilies, which thrive on the extra moisture. What with the midsummer's afternoon breeze blowing through the high pine woods and the fragrance of the lilies, it's a lovely spot for a leisurely bath.

One June afternoon, though, I came home to find Mama in a state. "Surprise is not something you hope for in a bath," she said grimly.

"What kind of surprise?" I asked.

"Bicyclists!" she said. "Hundreds of them, swarming through the yard like mayflies!"

It seemed Mama had been having her usual afternoon bath when suddenly, as if by magic, the yard was filled with bicyclists, angling gracefully around the curves of the flowerbeds, gliding effortlessly with flexed elbows over humps in the driveway, and swerving through the lilies, their thin tires leaving no trace. They were the serious kind, Mama said, with the skin-tight striped nylon costumes, black fingerless gloves, goggles, and enormous calves above short, thin socks. My mother is not as agile in the bathtub as she once was, and she wisely decided against desperate springs for the towel and fumbled efforts to cover herself with the Ivory soap and the washrag. Instead, she sat as still as she could, assuming an attitude of mingled wisdom and patience. Anyway, it didn't last long, she said. As quickly as they had come, they were gone, coasting with rumps aloft, down the hill in front of our house and disappearing into the thick woods that border a big cypress swamp.

Mama waited all afternoon for them to emerge, and by nightfall she was worried. That swamp, a small cousin of the Okefenokee, is a vicious place on a summer night. "When I think of the redbugs under those nylon tights . . . ," she said, and shuddered as she peered into the premature dusk of the swamp. "Remember Mr. Tate!" I don't remember Mr. Tate, but the story is that he got lost in the swamp and died of a combination of insect bites and briar scratches.

It's been months now, and there has been no sign of the bicyclists. My mother, who has an ability to create logic out of nothing, has convinced us that only her presence in the bathtub will bring them out. So even in the dead of winter, she bathes out there every afternoon. A column of steam rises steadily out of the bathtub and drifts over the tangled, frozen lily bed. She sits up straight and peers out through the steam at the early dusk. After a while she climbs out and comes in the house. "Maybe in the spring," she says. And already we can see the red noses of next year's lilies poking up through the straw.

Birth of the Blues

My mother and I disagree about music. Baroque is my favorite. I love the Goldberg Variations. "Too much toodle-te-toodle-te," Mama says. But she indulges me, and when I'm at home we listen to the classical music station. But the minute I'm out the door in the morning, she's up spinning the knob to 106.2, country and western.

When I get home from work in the evening, we sit out on the porch and eat bread and butter and drink tea. She rears back in her reclining chair and sings me the best songs she's heard that day. They are all about the wretchedness of love, the fickleness of women, and the strength of a good man. She has a deep voice and doesn't even try for the high notes. And when she can't remember the words, she just makes up something better. "Now that's good music," she says. I can't disagree.

There's one day she doesn't change the station when I leave the house, though. That's the day they have Listener Request on the classical music station. Every Thursday morning she's on the long-distance phone. My mother has an authoritative manner and an economical telephone delivery.

"Play me 'The Birth of the Blues' with Benny Goodman and his orchestra," she tells the little man at the radio station.

"I'm sorry, sir," says the man, "but we played that last week."

"Play it again," she says.

"Actually," says the man firmly, " 'The Birth of the Blues' is not classical music."

"It is to me," says Mama. "This is 'Listener Request.' I'm a listener. Play it." And he has to do it.

"You know, we've got a Benny Goodman record," I tell her. "Why don't you play the record and leave them alone at the radio station?"

"People need to hear 'The Birth of the Blues,' " she says. "It does them good."

On the first day of summer the classical music station plays a countdown of the top forty listener requests for that year. They start off at 9:00 A.M. with number forty, "The Sounds of Construction and Progress," by Kimio Eto, and work their way down. By afternoon they're in the teens: Mozart's Concerto for Flute and Harp, and Schubert's String Quintet in

C Major. At 5:00 P.M. all the faithful listeners are gathered round to hear the big three: Pachelbel's Canon in D, Vivaldi's Four Seasons, and then the number-one hit of this year, and every year since Mama discovered "Listener Request": "The Birth of the Blues," with Benny Goodman and his orchestra. Mama leans back in her chair and sighs. I don't dare move or breathe until it's over. "Now that's good music," she says.

Something Like a Husband

Because of a plumbing disaster under the house, we found that our telephone jack had to be moved. My mother called the telephone company, but the woman she talked to there wasn't encouraging. "It'll cost you eighty dollars for me to send a man out there to move that jack," she said. "Don't you have something like a husband who could do it for you?" Mama said she'd think about it, and hung up.

"Here we are, a widow and a spinster," I told Mama, "and she wants to know if we've got something like a husband."

"Well," said Mama, "we've got Howard."

Howard is our fifteen-year-old canary, who had lived all his life in silence until one morning last spring he rose up on his little bandy legs, stretched out his little bald neck, and screeched, "Bleech!"

"Howard's nothing like a husband," I said.

But Mama has had more experience with these things than I. She gave Howard a look. He flung some bird seed around in his cage. "You never know," she said darkly.

I knew in the end I would have to go under the house and move the telephone jack. It wasn't the drilling or the wiring that worried me. It was the spiders. There's a race of giant spiders living under our house—the kind with those high, knobby knees and that scrambling gait. I have a horror that one of those spiders will come out from under the house and crawl on me. So I decided we didn't really need a telephone, not for a few days at least.

It was during this time that we found, one afternoon, an enormous egg on our kitchen counter. It had been carefully propped against a jar lid so it wouldn't roll off, in among some dish towels, cookbooks, and jars of spices. I've seen goose eggs, swan eggs, and peacock eggs. But this was bigger than any other egg I'd ever seen. Mama held it in both hands and examined it.

"Where could it have come from?" she asked.

"Uncle Louis?" I said. My uncle Louis has made avian husbandry his life's work. For a while he raised guinea hens and sold them to cruise ships, where they were served up as "pheasant under glass." Then he raised quail on stacked wire racks. Every Monday a new brood of quail would hatch in the incubator, and he would move all the birds up a tier and put the new chicks on the bottom rack. The quail that had reached the top rack would be killed and butchered, packaged, and sold to grocery stores. It was all very neat and scientific. But in the end he settled down with white leghorn chickens and a feed-and-seed mill. "Maybe Louis is experimenting again," I suggested.

Mama weighed the egg in her hand. "Ostriches?" she guessed. "He's going to sell them to airlines as 'steak on the wing'?"

"Or Peter Verhoeven," I ventured. Verhoeven is an ornithologist at the biological experiment station down the road. But his specialty is woodpeckers, and this was no woodpecker egg.

Mama shot me a glare. "If we had a telephone," she said, "we could call around and ask."

But we didn't have a telephone. The only thing to do was to get Uncle Louis's old quail egg incubator out of the attic and fire it up. Mama did some research, and we set the heat halfway between the incubation temperature required for ostriches and swans. Then there was nothing to do but wait.

Mama invented a machine out of a shoe box and a light bulb with which she could monitor the progress of the egg. At first we could just see a red spot and spidery veins. A few days later a little embryo appeared, something like a cashew nut. In a week a giant eye floated into view. After that, all we could see was a huge shadow in the egg, dark and full. I began to have nightmares about spiders the size of baby ducks scampering under the bedclothes and birds with fierce, dark eyes and giant, pumped-up thighs at shoulder height dancing out of the dark. We kept waiting for a cheerful relative or scientist to drive up into the yard and announce gleefully, "It was me! I left that egg on your kitchen counter!" But no uncles or ornithologists showed up.

And after two weeks I finally gave up on finding something like a husband. "After all these years," Mama said, "I'd say our chances are pretty slim." I put on high-topped boots laced up tight, a turtleneck shirt, and a ski mask and crawled under the house with a roll of telephone wire, a pair of pliers, and a stapler. It was no mean trick doing the wiring with those mittens on. But I managed it and crawled out, batting spiders into the shadows. I could hear a thud as they hit the floor joists, then a scuttling sound, then, worst of all, the silence of spiders.

I felt pretty proud when I came back out into the sunlight. I stood up, brushed myself off—and right then the telephone rang. Howard rose up on his perch. "Bleech!" he screeched triumphantly.

"Shut up, Howard," I said.

Mama answered the phone.

"Nobody's talking," she said.

"Oh no," I thought. "It's not fixed after all."

"Wait!" said Mama, "I hear something: breathing—heavy breathing."

"Hang up, Mama!" I said. "You're supposed to hang up when you hear that."

"Wait," said Mama. "He's talking."

She listened a while. Then: "Yes. Absolutely. The biggest I've ever seen. It was you!" she crowed. "It was you who left that egg! Who is this?"

"Mama, he's not talking about our egg! Hang up!" I pleaded.

"Hot?" said Mama. "Well, we're keeping it right on 102. . . . Ten inches? No, it's nowhere near that big. I'd say four and a half inches, tops. Just tell me one thing: Is it an emu? Hello? Hello?

"He's gone," she said. "He said, 'Shit, lady,' and then he just hung up."

"*You* are the one who's supposed to hang up, Mama," I said. "You're supposed to blow a loud whistle and then hang up."

Mama thought for a while. "I hated to hang up on him. Poor thing," she said wistfully. "For a minute there, he sounded something like a husband."

Camping

I once talked my mother into knitting me a sweater out of some special unscoured wool I had brought back from a trip to the mountains. She didn't like it. "It stinks!" she complained, holding the hanks of yarn at arm's length. "It smells like goat pee!"

"Just hold your nose and knit," I pleaded. And she sighed, adjusted her glasses, and began casting on stitches.

My little four-year-old niece, Lucy, started hanging around our house. She wanted to learn to knit. "You're too young," Mama told her. "Your hands aren't big enough."

But Lucy was fascinated by the clicking needles. She leaned on her grandmother's knee and thought for a while. "My baby doll knows how to knit," she said. She paused, just long enough; then she gave Mama a shrewd glance. "Her grandmother taught her how to knit."

So Mama had to teach Lucy how to knit. They sat for hours, side by side. After a week Lucy had a six-inch-square knitted rag, filthy dirty and riddled with holes. Eventually Mama finished my sweater. Her hands were shiny from the lanolin.

One afternoon when my sister, Louise, came over to get Lucy, she brought Mama a book, *Naked Lunch*. "You've got to read this," she said. "It's due at the library in a week. I'll give you two days."

The next morning my cousin Sophie, a fundamentalist Christian, came to help me wash our kitchen. We do it every year. We move all the furniture out into the yard and scrub the ceiling, the walls, and the floor. We moved Mama's reclining chair out under the oak tree. She sat out there and read *Naked Lunch* all day. When we finished in the kitchen, Sophie strolled out to the oak tree to talk to Mama about Armageddon.

"Aunt Lila, I couldn't help noticing that you're sitting out here reading a novel. If you have time to read, don't you think you should be reading the Bible?" she said.

That night Louise came to get her book. We sat in the sparkling clean kitchen. Mama's lap looked strangely empty.

"Girls," she said, "I have an announcement to make."

We sat up. She never makes announcements.

"I'm going camping," she said.

"Camping!" we wailed.

"You're too old and feeble!" said Louise.

I, more tactful, but less to the point, grasped at straws. "And you don't have a tent!"

"I'm tired," Mama said firmly. "I'm tired of breathing the essence of a sheep fold; I'm tired of teaching babies to knit; I'm tired of being set upon by crazed Christians one minute and unbridled libertines the next. Girls, I'm going camping."

And she packed up her grandson's cowboy sleeping bag, her walking stick, matches, food, and all four volumes of *The Cyclopedia of American Horticulture* by L. H. Bailey.

"How long are you going to stay?" Louise and I asked, eyeing the stack of books and wringing our hands.

"Just as long as I want to," she said.

And off she went. After a few days I figured out where she had set up camp. At night I could see a tiny glow from her fire. And just at dawn, if I went out to the edge of the pasture and listened very carefully I could barely hear her singing "Meet Me in St. Louis."

Dead on the Road

My mother eats things she finds dead on the road. Her standards are high. She claims she won't eat anything that's not a fresh kill. But I don't trust her. I require documentation. I won't eat it unless she can tell me the model and tag number of the car that struck it.

Mama is an adventurous and excellent cook, and we have feasted not only on doves, turkeys, and quail, but robins, squirrels, and, only once, a possum. I draw the line at snakes. "But it was still wiggling when I got there," she argues. "Let's try it just this once. I have a white sauce with dill and mustard."

"No snakes," I say.

And she won't even slow down for armadillos,

although they are the most common dead animal on the road these days. "They look too stupid to eat," she says.

We have a prissy aunt Eleanor who comes to dinner every third Friday. We always get out the linen and polish the silver when she comes. She expects it. Last month we sat her down to an elegant meal, complete with the Spode china and camellias in a crystal bowl.

"The quail are delicious," my aunt sighed. "And I haven't found a single piece of shot. How do you manage it?"

"Intersection of 93 and Baggs Road," recites Mama. "Green late model pickup, Florida tag. Have another one. And some rice, El."

Nonrepresentational Art

My sister, Louise, thinks our mother should get out more, broaden her views, and lead a rich, full life. I myself am content to let her sit in her reclining chair all day, reading the UFO newsletter, listening to the radio, and drawing conclusions. For one thing, it's hard for her to get around, and for another, she startles people sometimes with her blood-curdling solutions for the world's problems.

So it was my sister's idea for us all to go to supper at the house of an artist friend of hers, and afterward to an opening at an art gallery where one of his paintings was part of a juried exhibit.

Louise, who is a great believer in the benefits of physical exercise, had the idea that it would be a pleasant excursion for us to walk from her house across Tallahassee to her friend's house. She had even gone so far as to rent a wheelchair for our mother, who can walk, but not that far and not at the pace my sister thinks provides the most aerobic benefit. We settled Mama into the wheelchair and loaded her down with both our pocketbooks and a vase of flowers I had picked to present to our host in hopes of softening the effects of any opinions Mama might vent during the evening. Louise got a grip on the handles, and off we went.

Tallahassee is an Indian word meaning "City of Seven Hills." Louise set the pace at what I considered breakneck speed—a "fitness walk" she called it. Mama hung on to the armrests of the wheelchair with both hands and clamped the vase of flowers between her knees. Every block or so I would sprint around to the front of the chair to see how she was doing. Her little face peered out grimly from behind the bobbing daisies, and her knuckles were white. Every time Louise would swoop her down one of those wheelchair-accessible curbs, a dollop of water would fly out of the vase and plop into her lap.

About halfway there Louise began giving Mama a breathless little preparatory lecture on the sort of art we were likely to see.

"What?" shouted Mama. "I can't hear you with this wind whistling around my ears."

"Nonrepresentational art!" my sister repeated.

Mama's favorite pictures are all of cows— Holstein or Jersey cows in sunny fields.

"That means no cows, Mama!" I yelled.

"Or if there are cows, you won't be able to tell it," Louise explained, puffing up the seventh hill.

We arrived. Mama rose from the wheelchair and swept up to the door with her walking stick in full play. Louise and I hung back to catch our breath and straighten our clothing. Mama handed our host the flowers and said, "My daughters are maniacs."

Supper was elegant, but not substantial—little dabs of pink-and-white food on lettuce leaves. Mama pulled a saltshaker out of her pocket and gave everything on her plate a heavy sprinkling. The artist-host watched, mesmerized. It was like a little snowstorm.

On the way to the gallery Mama sat in the front with our host, and Louise and I sat in back. Mama was telling him all about Holstein cows. We were proud to see that his picture had won first place. It was a small watercolor, with streaks of light green and tan. It might have been a tiger in sunlight, but this being Florida, I thought more of a palmetto frond. Louise and I looked carefully at all the pictures. Then we wandered out onto the porch, where we found Mama and the artist sitting in chairs and talking.

I could tell from the fully present look of the top of his glowing bald head that Mama was describing her invention of a cure for male-pattern baldness. She calls it "the axillary transplant." After a while we all headed back to Louise's house. The artist seemed a little distracted as he helped us unload Mama's wheelchair and then shook her hand. We told him good-night, and congratulations.

Driving Mama home from my sister's house, I wondered what that nonrepresentational artist would dream about that night as he lay in bed with the top of his head tingling. Probably he would dream about his prize-winning painting at the art gallery. But just maybe in his dreams, those dim green-and-tan vegetable tigers will melt away, and in their place will stand a herd of Holsteins in a sunny field, with all the light and all the shadows in the world seeping out of the black and white of those cows.

I can't wait for his next exhibit.

The Bed

A secret door, a dimly lit flagstone passage, echoing footsteps where no feet ought to be, a hollow murmur, a gust of wind, an extinguished candle . . .

In these days when "helpless heroine" is an oxymoron and no deeds are nameless, it's hard to take those old Gothic novels seriously. If you'd ever spent a night in our house, however, with my old mother and me, you might feel differently.

In those books the interest eventually settles on a piece of furniture or a fantastical element of architecture—a heavy-lidded chest, a locked drawer in an ormolu cabinet, a ruined chapel, or a sliding panel behind a gloomy tapestry. In our house it is a bed—a huge bed, dark oak, with some swampy-looking vegetation dimly depicted in bas relief on the headboard. An old aunt of mine temporarily took leave of her senses in 1890-something and went out and bought it. Her sanity returned soon afterward, but by then it was too late. Forty-five strong men had delivered the bed and had set it up in the guest room.

And it is not only a bed: by means of a series of hair triggers and precisely balanced weights and counterweights it can be made to swing up and fold itself into its headboard to reveal on the underside, now nearly vertical, an enormous beveled mirror. The two little iron legs at what was the foot of the bed can then be folded into neat grooves specially made for them, and there, through the dust and cobwebs on the glass, your own reflection peers dimly out at you.

However, as you might imagine, in neither position is the thing satisfactory as a piece of furniture. In the mirror position the top leans out slightly, as if it were yearning to unfold itself and become a bed again, so that your image appears as a monster with a huge watermelon-sized head and dwindles down to a pair of tiny, remote feet almost hidden in the shadows. And as a bed it seems always to be on the verge of becoming a mirror, with the weights and counterweights groaning and the two iron legs at the foot lifting themselves ever so slightly off the floor. There's no room for springs, so the wafer-thin mattress lies on a steel net of something that looks like chain mail stretched across the frame. Over the years sprongs of steel have popped loose and snagged the mattress ticking to reveal the horse-hair stuffing. I've noticed that the hair is all the same color. This, combined with the extreme thinness of the mattress, has led me to conclude that the hair all came from just one horse. The oppressive size, the dark color of the oak, and the steel sprongs have made bedtime a dreaded moment for guests in my family for nearly one hundred years.

But the worst part is the tendency the bed has in the dead of night when all is quiet in the house, to transmogrify itself into a mirror. Some mysterious atmospheric change will release a catch somewhere, and slowly and majestically the foot of the bed will begin to rise. The weights and counterweights mutter to each other, the old oak joints creak and groan, and the mirror reveals its phantasmagoric images to the night as it lifts itself upright. The poor guest wakes out of a strange dream to find the covers bunched on his chest, all his blood settling at his head, and his bare, drained, ice-cold feet pointing to the ceiling. It's hard to recover from this position in the dark of night in a strange house, and usually the guest falls into a trancelike swoon that lasts until morning, when Mama discovers his predicament, snatches the foot of the bed down again, briskly clicks the latch back into position, and says, "We should have warned you about the bed."

Half an hour later the poor fellow will stagger

out, hollow eyed and grim, suitcase packed, and catch an early train home, never to return.

Over the years the word must have spread. No one comes to visit us now. We just live here all alone, my mother and I, like Briar Rose behind her hedge of thorns.

This evening, though, we got a telephone call. A distant cousin from Philadelphia whom we've never met is passing through on her way to Florida. "I want to stay with my old relations," she tells Mama on the telephone.

It is dusk. I hear the wind soughing through the pine trees as I take clean sheets into the guest room. The light from the twenty-watt bulb dangling on its cord from the vaulted ceiling barely reaches the edges of the room. The dark draperies sway against the windows.

"I've heard so much about Southern hospitality," the cousin chirps on the telephone. "Now I will be able to experience it for myself."

From far away I hear the rumble of thunder. Or is it the lead weights in the bed beginning their groaning chorus of the night? "We will expect you in a half hour," Mama says confidently. "You are welcome to stay as long as you like."

Family Ghosts

The Monkeys Not Seen

My grandfather was not a faithful correspondent. His sister, who had married and moved to New Jersey, wrote to him regularly. She wanted the news of home, and she was so annoyed by his lack of response that she sent him a monkey in the mail. My grandfather hated monkeys, but he was not a cruel man, and he built a cage for the monkey in the shade of a magnolia tree and cared for it very properly all its long life.

There was a boy who lived about eighty miles away in the little fishing town of Carrabelle, on the north Florida coast, who had never seen a monkey. But he wanted to see one. Carrabelle was a primitive little place, and except for a great variety of fish and fish bait, there wasn't much to see there.

This boy's longing had reached such a pitch that you could almost say that it was his life's wish to see a monkey. My grandfather, hearing of his desire, drove all the way down to Carrabelle on muddy roads in a Model A Ford roadster to get that boy and bring him up into Georgia to see the monkey.

The boy sat in the rumble seat. They rode and rode through the scrub pines and palmetto woods, past the little fishing hamlets of Panacea and St. Marks. But when they got to the outskirts of Tallahassee, then a good-sized town, the boy saw a bicycle. He got so excited that he threw up all in the rumble seat. He threw up and threw up until he was so exhausted and dehydrated that my grandfather had to turn the car around and take the boy back to Carrabelle. He never did see the monkey. But for the rest of his life he haunted the docks and the bait stores of Carrabelle, a pale, wraithlike creature with fluttering hands and a radiant look in his eyes, telling everybody who would listen about the time he almost saw a monkey.

In the meantime, the monkey huddled, scruffy and irritable in its cage, its wizened little face peering out with dull eyes at a world where it was not at home.

But what a glorious creature that boy must have imagined all those years—what flashing eyes and shimmering fur, a tail that could do almost anything.

And, perhaps, a long, narrow, intelligent hand reaching through the wire of the cage and across the gap to touch him gently on the cheek.

The very best and finest monkeys, the monkeys that bring you the purest joy—those are the monkeys you must never see.

The Inn

My ancestral home—one of those magnificent Greek revival houses with the Doric columns, the hand-carved rosette of laurel leaves in the pediment, and the avenue of oak trees—has become an inn.

Over the generations my family has metastasized from that high hill to lower spots all over the county. Once members of the leisure class, we are now farmers, carpenters, teachers, and mechanics. My uncle Louis was the last member of the family to own the house, and he found that maintaining it in the style to which the National Trust for Historic Places thought it was entitled was costing him more than raising his three daughters. So he sold it to a tough-looking Scandinavian woman, and within weeks she had turned every other bedroom into two bathrooms, planted some scraggly rosebushes on each side of a concrete sign with the house's name gouged out in fancy script, and opened it up as an inn.

No one told her until the last papers had been signed that the house was haunted. The ghosts are not the ordinary kind—no doors creaking in the night or dogs watching the progress of nothing steadily mounting the circular staircase. These were eating ghosts. On nights near the solstices, people in the house would be awakened by the sounds of slurping, smacking, crunching, and the clink of cutlery. In the morning, something would be missing from the kitchen—a box of shortbread, a ham bone, a jar of artichoke pickles. And in my great-grandmother's garden there would be wide, winding, silvery trails in the dew, something like the tracks of giant slugs.

The day before the inn opened up for business, Miss Bergheim invited my mother and me and all my aunts and uncles for supper. It was a goodwill gesture. We stood around awkwardly. The furniture looked unsettled. Miss Bergheim's father sat bolt upright on a high-backed mission-style chair. He knew we didn't speak his language, so he thoughtfully limited himself to two words: "ja" and "snö." By varying his inflection, he managed quite a lively conversation.

Miss Bergheim was not a good hostess, and no

one could eat her cooking. Her procedure in the kitchen was to arrange the food stingily and artistically on black plates, pour a half cup of hard liquor over everything, strike a match, and there's your supper. Louis, a recovering alcoholic, had to leave the room, and my aunt Belle singed her eyebrows on a quarter of a banana. I tried to be cheerful and made conversation as best I could.

"Has anyone heard the ghosts?" I asked.

Miss Bergheim fixed me with a gaze as blue as an iceberg. "Ghosts? No."

After supper we stayed only a little while. My mother had brought the family photograph album with pictures of the house in earlier days, and we showed Mr. Bergheim the black-and-white photograph (mostly black) taken on December 15, 1958, the day it had snowed. "Ja," he said, pointing at the picture and nodding his head encouragingly. "Ja, snö, snö."

Conversation was not charitable on the drive home. Uncle Jimbuddy, a fine cabinet maker, was offended by the furniture.

"Imitation Spanish inquisition!" he wailed, clutching his head in both hands. "Those knobs, like the testicles of massacred heretics!"

"Of course she doesn't hear the ghosts," Aunt Belle snapped. "She's starved them to death."

The inn did not prosper, and my family greeted the rumors of every setback with relish. I thought it cruel of them, and I stood up for Miss Bergheim whenever I could. It didn't seem to help.

Down at Castleberry's store early one cold Saturday morning, I ran into several of my aunts. They were hanging over the counter and whispering to Mae Castleberry. I could tell by the earnest arch of their eyebrows that Miss Bergheim was the topic of conversation. Sure enough, she had just been in, buying instant coffee, toilet paper, and a can of sardines.

"For her guests!" hissed Mae.

"Sardines for breakfast!"

"But," I said, "maybe she makes some delicious Scandinavian cream sauce." Instantly the eyebrows turned on me. "With dill or rosemary," I continued bravely.

The arches curled, and I began to waver. "On toast they might be . . ." One of each pair of eyes squinted shut. Lips pursed. The aunts turned back to Mae.

"On a cold day like this she should feed them hot sausage and eggs," said Aunt Eleanor.

"Grits and bacon."

"Biscuits and spoon bread."

"With redeye gravy!"

That afternoon I went over to the inn. I wanted the concrete-and-copper urn my great-grandmother had made as a garden ornament. I was nervous about asking, but I figured it was just crumbling away in the abandoned garden, and Miss Bergheim had no attachment to it. The weather continued cold. The high that day would only be in the sixties, and Mr. Bergheim was dressed up in his snowflake sweater, red suspenders, and worsted wool trousers. He was strolling up and down the green lawn, reeking of lanolin, cedar, and sweat. He pointed emphatically at one puffy cloud in the blue blue sky and nodded optimistically to me, "Snö, ja." A few pinched-looking guests eyed me suspiciously as I approached Miss Bergheim with my request.

"No," she said without a pause. "My guests like to walk in the old garden for the scenic view. You may not have it."

And that was that. My aunts were wild. Aunt Belle was all for stealing it. "I'll drive the getaway car," she said, her false teeth clacking. "We'll work out a series of secret signals. I'll signal to you when the coast is clear, you signal to me when you've got it, I'll rev her up, you throw it in the back, jump in, and we'll be off. She'll never miss it!"

But I didn't have the nerve. I could easily imagine Aunt Belle in her enthusiasm for the secret signals getting confused and roaring off into the night, leaving me clutching the urn as four of Miss Bergheim's giant Alsatians loped toward me, snarling and slobbering, and Miss Bergheim herself glided across the lawn after them with her icy stare.

And it's just as well. Those ornaments properly belong in the clipped, constipated gardens of a hundred years ago, with their neatly edged, perfectly round rose beds and tidy boxwood borders. Mine is a garden of the 1990s—a tangled half-acre of wild-flowers and herbs.

The other night, though, we had a surprise: visitors.

"Did you hear it?" I asked my mother in the morning.

"Smacking," she said.

"The scrape of knives and forks," I said.

"What's missing?"

We looked through the pantry. Only two plum puddings. We were positive there had been three. I ran out to my garden. Sure enough, through the goldenrod and artemisia the trails went winding, all streaked with silver. The ghosts, at least, have found their way home.

The Devil's Hoofprints

 "Where are we?" I asked Aunt Belle.

"I'm sure we're almost there," she said.

"I know," I said, "but where is that?"

We were meandering along a back road some-where near Bath, North Carolina. It was 1960-something. My aunt was driving. I was holding a big red chicken on my lap. We were looking for the Devil's Hoofprints. "The Devil's Hoofprints, near Bath, North Carolina" was all the booklet had said: "Dirt will not fill these strange depressions, and chickens will not eat out of them."

"We're almost there," Aunt Belle said. "I can feel it. Get that chicken feed out of the backseat."

"Junkets" my aunt called these summertime wanderings of ours. Last summer it had been fossil hunting in Virginia. This year we were ferrying our way through North Carolina. Aunt Belle had a taste for the peculiar and the exotic:

WORLD'S SMALLEST HORSES

SEE A LIVE PERFORMING BEAR

GHOST OF BLACKBEARD HAUNTS OUTER BANKS

"Unexplained mysteries" were a favorite theme. She also loved thunderstorms, wheat fields, and ferry-boats. And even if the world's smallest horse turned out to be an ill-tempered, medium-sized Shetland pony, and the bear's only trick was to stand upright and make a slow twirl, shedding great rags of fur all the while, and the ghost of Blackbeard was discovered to be nothing but lightning bugs, she was never disappointed. She just banked up more enthusiasm for the next adventure.

Before we had left on this trip, Aunt Belle had taken the map and marked with a red star every place name in the whole state of North Carolina containing the word *ferry*, and we had spent all of July aimlessly crossing and recrossing rivers and inlets on ferryboats. The only problem was, many towns, like Hadley Ferry and Crawford's Ferry, no longer have operating ferries. In these towns, after some searching along the waterfront, I would be sent to ask.

I was in the throes of adolescence that summer, suffering from a paralyzing shyness, and my main goal in life was to be not noticed. My aunt would park across the street from a knot of rough-looking men lounging outside the feed store, and I would shuffle over to them with my shoulders hunched up to my ears and my hands in my pockets.

"Um. Where's the ferry?" I would whisper.

"Ferry?" they would hoot. "*Ferry?*" Then they would call some other men out from the back of the store. "This here girl's looking for the ferry!" They would slap each other and double over laughing.

"Ain't been no ferry here for fifty years, girl," they would say, drying their eyes. They would straighten up and look me over. My ears would begin to ring. Then would come the inevitable question: "Where you trying to get to, honey?"

"Well," I would say, gulping, "we're not really trying to get to anywhere."

Big goofy grins would spread over their faces, and I would try to blend in with the air.

"My aunt just wants to ride the ferry."

"Well, she ain't gon' ride no ferry here," one of the men would howl, and I would creep back across the street to a chorus of snorting and hollering. "She sho' ain't gon' ride no ferry here!"

It was while we were looking for one of those vanished ferries that Aunt Belle learned about the Devil's Hoofprints. People had been trying to fill the holes since 1813, when they first appeared, but they always came back, each one six inches deep and the size of a dinnerplate.

I kept trying to distract her, because I knew that

somewhere down the line I was going to have to buy a live chicken from a local farmer. "How about this?" I said, reading from our guidebook. "Oldest Episcopal church in North Carolina, right in Bath. Why don't you want to go see that church?"

"Chickens will not eat out of those hoofprints," she mused. "Imagine that. Look!" she crowed. "There's a man with a nice garden. I know he's got some chickens around back." She pulled the car onto the shoulder of the road. "Go ask him."

"Do you want it picked and cleaned?" asked the farmer, eyeing me suspiciously.

"No, just a plain chicken. A live chicken," I mumbled.

He looked at me for a long time. My ears began to ring. But in the end I did get the chicken, a big Rhode Island Red hen with a steely glint in her eye and a surly disposition.

"I'm sure we're almost there," Aunt Belle said, and she turned down a little lane into an old pine hammock. Straw was thick on the ground, but after some rooting around, we found them—twelve in all, just as the booklet had said, the size of dinner-plates. My aunt sprinkled a handful of chicken feed in each depression, plus one handful on the side. "That's our control," she said. "We've got to be scientific. Now put that chicken down." She stood back to observe, and I set the old hen on the ground and stepped aside.

The hen squatted there for a minute, then she

puffed herself up with a little growl, gave us each a beady-eyed glare, and stalked off into the woods. Pretty soon she was out of sight. We stood there for a moment. Then my aunt said optimistically, "Well, she didn't eat out of them." We gathered up the chicken feed, and after a little fruitless searching for the chicken in the thickets, we drove off.

And that's all I remember from my ferrying summer in North Carolina almost thirty years ago. Aunt Belle died last year, and at her funeral, as the priest droned on about being joined with blessed saints in glory everlasting, and eternal life, I said to myself, I don't know where she's trying to get to, but I'm sure she's almost there. And I hope, someday soon, a little niece will be traveling with her aunt on the back roads of North Carolina, and they'll read in a newsprint booklet somewhere:

FERAL CHICKENS DISCOVERED IN N.C.

No one knows the origin of these mysterious birds, discovered near Bath, North Carolina. Wary and elusive, the giant red chickens have been spotted on moonlit nights . . .

Bluebirds

Every Friday night my mother and I go to eat at the catfish restaurant down the road. We don't really like catfish that much, but my Uncle Sonny eats there on Friday nights, and we really go there just to hear him talk. Uncle Sonny is a retired logging man, and he knows a lot about the woods and what's in them.

I always take one of the Palliser novels when we go to the catfish restaurant, because on some nights Mama and Uncle Sonny get into a fiery dispute about whether some kind of tree Uncle Sonny calls wahoo is really *Viburnum prunifolium* or one of the haws. Mama doesn't have any patience with common names. She likes genus and species. Eyes flash and catfish bones fly, and they can keep it up until the waitresses are all wandering around the empty tables flapping their rags, and Lady Glencora Palliser has given birth to an heir.

But on some nights I don't even open the book. Those are the nights when Uncle Sonny tells about his logging days. Last Friday he told about one winter evening when it snowed. It doesn't snow here much—just every twenty years or so—and when it does, we really appreciate it.

It was so very cold that night that Uncle Sonny had to get out of his warm bed and go out in the woods where he had his logging operation and drain the water out of his tractor and skidder.

It was a beautiful night, he said, the most beautiful night he's ever seen. The moon was full and the air was not moving, and the woods were bright with a kind of light Uncle Sonny had never seen before and quiet with a kind of stillness he had never heard before.

The next morning the snow melted and the sun shone down in the ordinary way. Uncle Sonny refilled his radiators and thought how his visit to the woods the night before might almost have been a dream. But the first tree he cut down that day was hollow, and in the hollow of that tree were stuffed the frozen dead bodies of dozens and dozens of bluebirds. They must have gone in there to try to keep warm, Uncle Sonny thinks.

On the way home from the catfish restaurant

that Friday night, Mama didn't talk about the viburnums. And when I got in bed, I didn't feel like finding out whether Plantagenet Palliser gets to be Chancellor of the Exchequer. I just lay in the dark and thought about that beautiful cold night and all those dead bluebirds.

Good Housekeeping

It was the middle of November, just a month before the wedding, when my mother announced that she was going to invite the family of our cousin's bride to Thanksgiving dinner at our house.

"They need to get to know us on our own ground," she said. She rared back in her reclining chair. "You girls can help with the cooking. Let's see, there will be ten of us, and six of those Mitchells" (the bride's family).

My mother was sitting in the kitchen, dammed in by stacks of old *Natural History* magazines. Behind her a bowl of giant worms, night crawlers, was suspended from the ceiling. She uses worm castings as an ingredient in her garden compost, and she keeps the worms in the kitchen so she can feed them food scraps.

My sister and I didn't say anything for a while. I watched the worms. Every now and then one of them would come up to the edge of the bowl, loop himself out, swag down—where he would hang for an instant, his coating of iridescent slime gleaming—and then drop down like an arrow into another bowl on the floor. My mother had an idea that the worms missed the excitement of a life in the wild, and she provided this skydiving opportunity as an antidote for boredom.

My sister was eyeing the jars of fleas on the kitchen counter, part of an ongoing experiment with lethal herbs.

Those worms, or their ancestors, had been there my whole life, but somehow, until this moment, it had not seemed odd to have a bowl of night crawlers getting their thrills in the kitchen.

"Worms," I whispered to myself.

"Fleas," my sister whispered.

My eyes fell on a rusty 1930s Underwood typewriter under the kitchen sink. It had been there as long as I could remember, the G key permanently depressed, the strike arm permanently erect. My sister and I exchanged a look.

"What is that typewriter doing under the sink?" I asked flatly.

"Why on our own ground?" said my sister.

"Let's see, we'll have your Aunt Thelma's sweet

potato crunch, and Corrie Lou's cranberry mold," my mother said.

Beside the typewriter was a guide to the vascular flora of the Carolinas, a turtle skull, and a dog brush. There were hairs in the dog brush, black hairs. Our dog Smut had died fifteen years ago. I thought about the typewriter, the turtle skull, and the dog brush. I thought about the worms. I thought about the bride's family—nice people, we were told, from Bartow County—walking into this house on Thanksgiving Day.

"Welcome to our home," my mother would say. And she would lead them over the stacks of books, through the musty main hall, and into a twilight of clutter. They would clamp their arms to their sides and creep behind her with their tight lips and furtive eyes, past rooms with half-closed doors through which they would glimpse mounds of moldy gourds, drying onions spread on sheets of newspaper, broken pottery in stacks, and, amazingly preserved, my grandfather's ship model collection. From one room a moth-eaten stuffed turkey would blindly leer out at them. "Storage!" my mother would explain cheerfully.

The guests would be settled on the front porch, where they would gaze hollowly down into the garden while our mother explained the life cycle of the solitary wasp who made his home in one of the porch columns. My sister and I would pass around plates of olives and cheese brightly, trying to keep a lilt in our voices and making the guests feel "at home."

"You can't do it!" my sister exploded. "We can never get ready in time!"

"What is there to get ready?" our mother asked innocently. "Just the food, and we'll do that ahead of time. You should always do the food ahead of time, girls," she instructed us. "Then you can enjoy your guests."

"Mama!" my sister wailed. "Just look at this place!" She gestured wildly.

"What's wrong with it?" My mother peered out at the room through a haze of dust. Behind her, another worm dropped.

"Just look!" Louise threw her arms wide. "The clutter, the filth . . ." She spied the rows of jars on the counter. ". . . The fleas!"

"Don't worry about the fleas, Louise," our mother reassured her. "I am working on a new concoction, based on myrtle and oil of pennyroyal. I may have the fleas under control by Thanksgiving."

Louise sank into a chair and looked our mother in the eye. "Mama," she began, "it's not just the fleas. It's . . ."

But I had come to my senses.

"Stop, Louise," I said. "Get up. We've got a weekend. We'll start on Saturday."

Louise arrived at dawn, the Saturday before Thanksgiving, loaded down with vacuum cleaners, extra bags and filters, brooms, mops, and buckets.

Mama was sitting in her chair in the kitchen, eating grits and making feeble protestations. "You girls don't have to do this, Bailey. I'll sweep up Wednesday afternoon. Then on Thursday there will just be the cooking."

"I know, Mama," I said, "but we want to do a good job. We want to really straighten up. You'll be glad when it's all done. Eat your grits." I didn't want her to see Louise staggering out with the first load for the dump: a box of rotten sheets, some deadly appliances from the early days of electricity, and an old mechanical milking machine with attachments for only three teats.

Mama would not let us throw out a box of old photographs we found under the sofa—"I may remember who those people are some day"—or the lecherous old stuffed turkey with his hunched-up back and his bad-looking feet. "It was one of Ralph's earliest taxidermy efforts," she said, fondly stroking the turkey's bristling feathers down. And she let us haul off boxes of back issues of the *Journal of the American Gourd Growers' Association* only if we promised to leave them stacked neatly beside the dumpster for others to find. But she got suspicious when she caught Louise with the typewriter.

"Where are you going with that typewriter, Louise?" she asked.

"We're going to throw it away, Mama."

"You can't throw it away, Louise. It's a very good typewriter!"

Louise was getting edgy. "Mama, it's frozen up with rust and clogged with dust. None of the moving parts moves. And they don't make ribbons to fit those old typewriters anymore."

"Nonsense," said Mama. "You put that typewriter down, Louise. It just needs a little squirt of oil. Bring me the WD-40."

Louise put the typewriter down with a *clunk*. I brought a can of WD-40, with the little red straw to aim the spray. Mama put on her glasses, pursed her lips, and peered into the typewriter. *Skeet! Skeet!* She went to work with the WD-40 and a tiny, filthy rag. "You girls are throwing away too much," she said.

By midafternoon we began to feel that we were making progress. We could see out the windows, and we had several rooms actually in order. We had found our brother's long-lost snakeskin collection and the shoes our great-aunt Bertie had worn at her wedding; a dusty aquarium containing the skeletons of two fish; and under a tangle of dried rooster-spur peppers and old sneakers, a rat trap with an exquisitely preserved rat skeleton, the tiny bright-white neck bones delicately pinched. "Just like Pompeii," Mama marveled.

By the end of the day we had cleared the house out. What had not been thrown away was in its place. I had dropped a drawer on my foot, and Louise was in a bad mood. Mama's glasses were misted with WD-40. We sat down in the kitchen and drank tea.

"What I want to know is, where are the priceless heirlooms?" asked Louise. "You read about people cleaning out their attics and finding 200-year-old quilts in perfect condition, old coins, cute kitchen appliances from the turn of the century, Victorian floral scenes made of the hair of loved ones. What kind of family are we? All we find is bones of dead animals and dried-up plants. Where are the Civil War memorabilia, the lost jewels, the silk wedding dresses neatly packed away in linen sheets and lavender?"

"Well," said Mama, "you found your brother's snakeskins. And I think this rat skeleton is fascinating. How long must it have been there?"

"Don't ask," moaned Louise. "I'm going home."

On Sunday we dusted everything, swept, vacuumed and mopped the floors, washed the windows, and laundered the curtains, rugs, and slipcovers. By nightfall the house was ready.

"You girls have certainly struck a blow," Mama congratulated us. "This place is as clean as a morgue." We left her sitting in her chair with the worms, the typewriter, and the last three surviving fleas.

I walked out with Louise. "She looks a little forlorn," I said.

"She'll get used to it," Louise declared. "And the Mitchells will never dream that we are peculiar!"

Thanksgiving morning. Louise and I divided up the cooking. She made the sweet potato soufflé and the squash casserole, and I cooked the turkey and made bread. Mama spent the morning in her garden picking every last English pea, even the tiniest baby ones, because we knew we would have our first freeze that night.

At ten o'clock we set the table. For a center-piece Mama put some pink and white sasanquas to float in a crystal bowl, and the low autumn light came slanting in through the windows onto the flowers and the bright water. We had built a fire in the stove, and the heat baked out the hay-field fragrance of the bunches of artemisia hung to dry against the walls. The floors gleamed. The polished silverware shone. Beneath the sweet fall smells of baking bread and sasanquas and drying herbs I could just detect the faintest whiff of Murphy Oil Soap. Louise and I stood in the middle of the living room and gazed.

"The furniture looks startled," Louise said.

"It's beautiful," I said. "And here they are."

"Welcome to our home. We're so glad you could come," Mama was saying to the Mitchells. "Come out onto the porch. You will be interested to see the wasp who lives there. It's a solitary wasp, quite rare . . . I know it looks a bit cleared out in here; my girls have been cleaning. Bailey, Louise, come and meet these Mitchells."

We sat on the porch for a while, bundled in coats, and watched the last petals of the sasanquas drift to the ground. Mr. Mitchell examined the neat, round hole of the solitary wasp with some interest.

"Do you have a knowledge of the hymenoptera, Mr. Mitchell?" Mama asked. And she was off.

Mrs. Mitchell had smiley eyes and a knowing look. She leaned over to Louise and me. "It's the cleanest house I've ever seen," she whispered. We were friends. Louise and I took her to the kitchen to help with the food.

Other guests arrived—our brother and his family, aunts and uncles, and the bridal couple. The house was full of talk and laughter. We brought out food and more food. Everyone sat down.

Then, "Where's Daddy?" asked the bride.

Sure enough, an empty chair... two empty chairs.

"Where's Mama?" asked Louise.

"On the porch?"

No.

"In the kitchen?"

No.

"Everyone please start. The food will get cold," I said. "I'll go find them."

Outside, the temperature was dropping. This was the last day the garden would be green. I wandered along the path, following the scent of bruised basil until I heard voices way in the back of the yard.

Mr. Mitchell: ". . . and this is?"

"*Franklinia altamaha*, Mr. Mitchell, and quite a spectacular specimen, if I do say so."

"The famous Lost Franklinia of John Bartram,"

Mr. Mitchell murmured reverently, gazing up into its branches. "I have never seen one."

The sun shining through the crimson leaves of the Franklinia lit up the air with a rosey glow. Mr. Mitchell was holding her arm in his and gesturing with her walking stick. She was cradling some stalks of red erythrina berries in their black pods.

Mr. Mitchell turned slowly and looked over the garden. "Silver bell, shadbush, euonymous, bloodroot, trillium"—he named them off. "Mrs. White, I've been collecting rare plants and heirloom seeds all my life, and I've never seen anything to equal this."

"It's an old lady's pleasure, Mr. Mitchell," said my mother. "Now wait till I take you to the dump and show you my bones. Louise threw them out," she whispered hoarsely, "but I know right where they are. We'll get them tomorrow, if you're interested. You will be kind enough not to mention it to my girls."

"It would be my extreme pleasure to see your collection of bones, Mrs. White," said Mr. Mitchell. And slowly he led her out of the pink glow and back to the party.

The next day Louise came over, and we went to sit in the kitchen and drink hot chocolate with Mama and congratulate ourselves on a job beautifully done. But Mama was not in her chair. There was a note on the kitchen table. It was typewritten. Every letter was clear and black and even.

> Sorry I missed you girls. Mr. Mitchell and I have gone on a little errand. Make yourselves some hot chocolate.
>
> Love,
> Mama

Summer Afternoon

We never taught my little niece Lucy how to read. It just seems like she always knew how. When she was a baby, and my sister, Louise, and I wanted to be left alone to talk or cook or sew or garden, we'd just prop her up with a book on her lap. It didn't even have to have pictures. She'd sit and read. Except for her getting the pages all gummy with whatever she was eating, we figured there was no harm done.

Lucy grew up to be a beautiful little girl, all pink and silver. The summer she turned six years old, my sister went to college. I would keep Lucy during the mornings when Louise went to her classes, and at midday we would all meet down at the pond and have a picnic lunch. It's a small pond, with tall, dark pine woods growing down to the very edge of the water all around it, so that floating in that pond on a raft or a little boat, you had the feeling you were connected to the sky by a shaft of light.

Louise was studying English literature that summer, and after lunch we would loll around on the dock and Lucy would read *Pride and Prejudice* to us. Lucy could read anything, of course, but she hadn't been alive long enough to understand most of *Pride and Prejudice*. Still, like a tiny little idiot savant, she unerringly got every inflection and intonation just right.

"Read me my favorite part, about 'angry people are not always wise,' " I would beg. And Lucy would sigh, and read:

> but angry people are not always wise; and in seeing him at last look somewhat nettled, she had all the success she expected. He was resolutely silent, however; and, from a determination of making him speak, she continued. . . .

The summer afternoon heat would bake out a sweet, dry, piney smell from the woods, the cicadas would repeat their chorus over and over, and then the alligators would come. First we would notice just one. Then another nose and pair of eyes would silently pop up, then another and another, until there would be four or five of them, so relaxed and lulled by the summer day that they would float high in the water in a ring around the dock, and the sun would dry their backs so we could see their skin change color from shiny black to dusky gray as the day went by.

At the end of that summer, Lucy went to first grade. Louise changed her course of study and was all the time reading William Burroughs and Thomas Pynchon. Just a few times that year, late in the afternoon, we would find time to walk down to the pond. But it was all different by then. There was a smell of damp, the alligators were not to be seen, and from the dark pine woods a cold wind would blow.

After that, it seemed like twenty years went by faster than one of those summer afternoons. Lucy grew up, studied physics, and moved to Atlanta, where she now has a job she tries to explain to us when she comes home for a flying visit. "The TEF analyzer generates swept sine waves that go through the sound system. Then I read the system characteristics in the form of a three-dimensional plot on the computer screen," she tells us.

"Let's take a walk," I suggest.

Lucy says she doesn't have time, but I talk her into it. We walk to the pond. "Remember how we used to make you read *Pride and Prejudice* out loud?" I ask.

We stand on the dock and look out over the water. Lucy is wearing long, narrow red boots and purple knit pants.

"It was a kind of child abuse, really," I say. "I'm sorry if we didn't let you have a normal childhood, Lucy."

"Yeah," she says, "y'all burned me out on the early British novel before I was seven years old." But she laughs. "I still remember your favorite part," she says, and she recites:

> Persuaded as Miss Bingley was that Darcy admired Elizabeth, this was not the best method of recommending herself; but angry people are not always wise . . .

"Look," I whisper. There's an alligator's eyes and nose. Then another one, and another, until, cold as it is on this early spring day, we are surrounded by them, their backs and tails just breaking the surface. The air is cold, but standing on the dock in the shaft of sunlight, I can almost imagine a summer afternoon.

Joe King

When I was a little girl, I used to pal around with an old horse trainer named Joe King. He worked for our rich neighbors down the road, the Sedgwicks, who lived in Cleveland and came to their Georgia home only in winter for the climate and the hunting.

In the fall and winter Joe King had to work hard. Everything had to be kept just so. There were the horses, the mules that pulled the hunting buggies, the harnesses, the barns, and the kennels full of bird dogs so high-strung and alert that they looked like they were made out of springs wound up too tight.

In October ryegrass seed would be sowed on the lawns and up and down the drive to the big house. After just one rain the seed would sprout, and the startling green of the ryegrass would look like a bright scar against the natural colors of fall—gray and brown and the pinkish tan of broomsedge.

The big house would be thrown open, silver would be polished, Oriental rugs would be dragged into the yard to air, and Joe King would trim up the horses and grease the axles of the hunting buggies. Millet and benne seed would be planted in clearings in the woods as bait for doves and quail. Everything would be put in order.

There would be a few days of cold. The trees would lose their leaves. Then one frosty morning the ground would be covered with fat, sluggish robins. "Winter's coming," Joe King would tell me. After that I wouldn't see him for a long time.

But in the spring and summer, when the Sedgwicks had gone back to Cleveland, everything would relax. The big house would be closed up, and the horses would loll around with one hind foot cocked up, swatting flies with their tails. Even the bird dogs would relax in their doghouses with their feet flopping over the edge. Almost every day Joe King would drive into our yard, I would climb into his rattly, powdery blue pickup truck, and he would take me down to the Sedgwick's place. There would be Tony, "my" horse, a horse so old he had been named for a contemporary of his from the silent movies. Tony would hang his head over my shoulder and flop his old bristly lips against my neck. "He's glad to see you," Joe King would say.

I would scramble up onto Tony's high, narrow back, and Joe King would swing up on his horse, a flighty, prancing, light-footed mare named Princess, imported from Kentucky, and we would set out. Tony would fix his bleary gaze on a point way down the road and get ready to move. He seemed to owe his powers of locomotion not to any current process of thought but to some dim memory of walking that would come drifting back to him across the years. The Kentucky princess would dance and prance around him, flicking her little feet out and darting her head up and down. Before we'd gone a mile, she'd be dripping sweat and froth. But Tony would still be staring down the road, plodding along with his stultifyingly economical gait, cool and dry.

For entertainment, and to soothe the mare, Joe King and I would sing songs to each other. My favorite of his went like this:

> William Matrimatoes
> He's a good fisherman
> Catches hens
> Put 'em in pens
> Wire bright
> Clock fell down
> Little mice run around
> Old dirty dishrag
> You spell out and go.

I would sing him songs I had learned out of my *Little Golden Songbook* at school. I liked one about robins. It told about a little boy seeing a robin tap-tap-tapping on the windowpane and how he knew then that spring had come.

"Humph," said Joe King. "Something wrong with that song. Sure is something wrong with that song." We couldn't figure it out. Still, it had a nice tune, and I liked the tap-tap-tapping part in the chorus.

Then one fall, just before the Sedgwicks came, Tony began to die. Joe King came and got me and drove me down there. Tony was standing in the pasture under a big oak tree. He was gazing at something far away, just like he did when he walked down the road, only now he wouldn't move. He didn't seem to be hurting anywhere. He just acted like slowness had finally overtaken him. When I put my hand under his mouth, he flapped his lips one time and blew out a little puff of air.

He stood there for four days, watching his long, peaceful life pass in review. Then, one morning he was dead. They brought out a tractor and put a chain around his neck and dragged him away. The little Kentucky mare went wild. She danced around and around the pasture with her head high and the whites of her eyes showing and her tail flying like a banner. Joe King caught her finally and held her still. He hugged her with one arm and me with the other. He hugged rough, just like you would hug a horse, with my head clamped against his side.

The mare stood up high on her feet and stared

down the road where they had dragged Tony. She was trembling and shaking. Then she lifted her head and gave out a high, blowing whistle. It was almost like a cry. Joe King slapped her on the shoulder. "He's gone," Joe King said. "He ain't never coming back." The horse whistled again, and Joe King gave her another comforting clap. "He's dead and gone, and you ain't never gon' see him no more."

Then, that very winter, Joe King died. My mother dressed me all up in white, and we went to the funeral. I had never been to a funeral before, and I was mesmerized by the spectacle of it. There was loud singing and hollering, and Joe King's sister threw herself into the coffin with him and had to be pulled away. When I looked at him, the fact that he was wearing clothes I'd never seen before seemed more surprising than the fact that he was dead.

Spring came and the Sedgwicks went back to Cleveland. But Joe King didn't drive up into our yard in his powdery blue pickup truck smelling like horses and saddles and axle grease and Prince Albert. That's when I really missed him for the first time.

And I still miss him. Every year, when the robins have flown back up north and the trees are showing their first green, I think about Joe King. I remember the elegant grieving of the Kentucky mare, and the eerie, high, blowing whistle she gave. That's how I would like to mourn. But I don't have that much style. Instead, I take a little walk in the spring sunshine, and I say to myself:

William Matrimatoes
He's a good fisherman
Catches hens
Put 'em in pens
Wire bright
Clock fell down
Little mice run around
Old dirty dishrag
You spell out and go.

Sleep and Prayer

One rainy fall evening Sophie, my fundamentalist Christian cousin, careened into our yard in her Volkswagen Beetle and told us that there was a hurricane watch out for our whole county. She was excited. It might be the closest thing to Armageddon she would ever see. She stayed just long enough to tell us what to do, then she scratched off to prepare herself.

I took all the precautions. I filled the bathtubs with water, put buckets under all the leaky spots in the roof, closed all the doors and windows, and turned on the radio. The watch was upgraded to a warning, the wind began to scream, and we could see the tops of the long-leafed pine trees doing a mad dance against the black sky. The dog and I plastered ourselves like cardboard cutouts up against a bearing wall in the middle of the house. But my mother, who is not afraid of anything, tottered out to her little bed on the screen porch as usual with her cup of Ovaltine and *Young Men in Spats*, by P. G. Wodehouse. "I'll come in if it gets too bad," she said.

It did get bad. The wind sounded like a train coming through a tunnel, and every minute or so I could hear a snap, a crack, and a crash as another tree went down. About midnight I decided I had to go check on Mama. Clinging to the walls like a terrified roach, I made my way through the house and opened the door to her porch just a crack. Her quilt had been blown off the bed and was sucked up against the screen. There she lay, like a lizard on a fan blade, the tattered sheet clutched under her chin. "Oh no," I thought, "she's too terrified to move. I'll encourage her." I crawled along the floor toward her bed. As I got close, I could hear above the yowling wind and crashing trees her steady and sonorous snore.

The next day it was all over. Hundreds of trees were toppled in the woods, and our big black-walnut tree was down in the backyard, but not one had touched the house. Mama came out and built a little fire on the ground and started peeling apples. I climbed through the tops of fallen trees the mile and a half to my cousin's house. It took two hours to get there.

Sophie was sitting on a tree limb, wringing her hands, and crying. And it was a pitiful sight. Her yard was like a giant wagon wheel, with her house as the hub. Every tree that could reach the house—eight in all—had fallen on it. She climbed her way back home with me and told us about it while Mama dished up applesauce and hoecake.

"All night I kneeled by the bed and prayed," Sophie sobbed. "And every time I'd say amen, Bap! another tree would hit the roof." Mama gave her a big dollop of applesauce.

People say it was the worst hurricane to hit here since 1941. We didn't have electricity for almost a month. But we got enough money selling the trees that had blown down to pay for a whole new roof for our house. My cousin moved in with us while she decided what to do about her place. She ended up having the whole thing bulldozed into a little pile, and then she moved to Atlanta.

I know it's not a good idea to make generalizations about theological issues, but for some people at least, I'm pretty sure sleep is more effective than prayer.

Alligator

I remember as a little child watching my aunt Belle's wide rump disappear into the cattails and marsh grass at the edge of a pond as she crawled on her hands and knees to meet a giant alligator face to face. She was taming him, she said. We children would wait high up on the bank with our eyes and mouths wide open, hoping that the alligator wouldn't eat her up, but not wanting to miss it if he did.

Finally Aunt Belle would get as close to him as she wanted, and they would stare at each other for some minutes. Then my aunt would jump up, wave her arms in the air, and shout, "Whoo!" With a tremendous leap and flop the alligator would throw himself into the water. The little drops from that splash would reach all the way to where we were standing, and my aunt would come up the bank drenched and exultant. "I have to show him who's boss," she would tell us.

Later, Aunt Belle taught that alligator to bellow on command. She would drive the truck down to the edge of the pond and gun the engine. We would sit in the back, craning our necks to see him coming. He would come fast across the pond, raising two diagonal waves behind him as he came. He would haul himself into the shallow water and get situated just right. His back was broad and black. His head was as wide as a single bed. His tail would disappear into the dark pond water. He was the biggest alligator anyone had ever seen.

Then my aunt would turn off the engine. We would all stop breathing. The alligator would swell up. He would lift his head, arch his tail, and bellow. The sound would come from deep inside. It was not loud, but it had a carrying quality. It was like a roar, but with more authority than a lion's roar. It was a sound you hear in your bones. If we were lucky, he would bellow ten times. Then Aunt Belle would throw him a dead chicken.

The day came when she could just walk down to the pond and look out across the water. The alligator would come surging up to the bank, crawl out, and bellow.

By this time he was very old. My aunt got old, too. Her children had all grown up. She got to where she was spending a lot of time down at the pond. She'd go down there and just sit on the bank. When the alligator saw her, he'd swim over and climb out. He never bellowed anymore. They would just sit and look at each other. After a while my aunt would walk back to the house. The alligator would swim out to where the water was deep and black, and float for a minute; then he'd just disappear, without even a ripple. That's how he did.

But one day he didn't come when Aunt Belle went to the pond. He didn't come the next day, or the day after. All that summer, Aunt Belle walked around and around the pond looking, listening, and sniffing. "Something as big as that, you'd know if he was dead, this hot weather," she'd say. Finally, she stopped going down to the pond.

But sometimes, on the nights of the full moon in springtime, I can hear an alligator bellow. It comes rolling up through the night. It's not loud, but it makes me sit up in bed and hold my breath. Sometimes I hear it ten times. It's a peaceful sound.

Finger

My Uncle Jimbuddy, the cabinet maker, has been cutting off pieces of his fingers for ten years now. The doctors always try to talk him into letting them reattach the severed pieces. "There will be some loss of use," they say, "but from a cosmetic standpoint . . ."

But Uncle Jimbuddy says, "Naa. It would be flopping around down there and, hell, I'd just cut it off again."

He has found that the next one to go is always the longest, so he hopes someday to get them all of a length. Then, he thinks, maybe he can leave them alone.

I'll never forget the first time Uncle Jimbuddy lost a finger. In those days I was not used to it, as I have become over the years, and it took me by surprise.

Earlier in the day he had called my mother from his shop. He had a bushel of Cathead Island oysters he wanted to give us. We headed straight to town, because Cathead oysters are the best—they come from way out and have none of that brackish taint you often find in bay oysters.

When we got there, though; Uncle Jimbuddy was nowhere to be seen. We could hear crashing and scrambling in the back. It was Jimbuddy's son, Ambrose. He was covered with sawdust, and his eyes peered out at us frantically through a cherry and walnut haze.

"Daddy cut his finger off," Ambrose said. "If I can find it within"—he looked at his watch—"ten minutes now, and get it to the hospital in that bucket of ice, they can sew it back on."

We helped him search. With a beautiful gesture, Ambrose described the arc he recalled the finger taking from the table saw through the air to—where? No one saw it land.

Uncle Jimbuddy does not keep a neat workshop. The bare light bulbs hanging from their wires are dimmed by layers of sawdust, and in the gloom we pawed through piles of scrap lumber, moldings, floppy sheets of veneer, and miscellaneous Queen Anne legs and Chippendale ball-and-claw feet salvaged from wrecked furniture. My mother delicately and systematically poked and shifted things with the tip of her walking stick. Ambrose wildly hurled debris and toppled stacks of lumber. I even turned on the table saw, cut off the tip of a piece of molding, and traced its passage through the air to its landing place. Nothing. The minutes ticked by and the ice began to melt. After thirty minutes we stood up. We looked at each other and shook our heads.

Ambrose drove off disconsolately to the hospital. Mama and I got in our car. It was one of those spontaneous moments of silence. I sat at the wheel and watched the gray November dusk and thought about Uncle Jimbuddy's hands—big, capable, comfortable hands. For sixty years they had had ten fingers; then, in the work of an instant, nine. Mama broke the silence. "Get out and get that sack of Cathead Island oysters."

"How can you think about oysters at a time like this?" I asked.

"I can always think about oysters," she said. "Besides, Jimbuddy wouldn't want us to mope around drooling and starving and let those oysters rot in their sack just because he cut his finger off. And while you're at it," she added, "dump that bucket of ice on them. No need to waste perfectly good ice."

We got home just about dark. Mama went to work at the kitchen-porch sink, opening oysters and eating them as fast as she could. She doesn't use a glove. She says it slows her down.

Then, sure enough, about ten oysters into the sack, she found it. "Why, it's your Uncle Jimbuddy's finger!" And it was. Drained pale, shriveled, and ice cold, it didn't look like any part of a man I loved. Mama examined it dispassionately. "Well, he'll never have to worry about this hangnail again," she said.

I called Jimbuddy's house. "Mama found your finger in her oysters," I told him. "How's the rest of you?" He said he was fine. He was sitting up in bed drinking Scotch and eating Cathead oysters. "What did she do with it?" he asked.

"She's just looking at it," I said.

"You know," Mama mused in the background, "considering Jimbuddy is such a skinny man, this finger has a lot of meat on it."

"What do you want her to do with it?" I asked Jimbuddy.

"I don't care what she does with it," he said. Then he added, as a cautionary afterthought, "Just don't let her eat it."

Scary Movies

I have a sick fancy that whatever I see at the movies is going to happen to me at home. My bladder capacity increased tenfold after I saw *The Shining*, because I was sure if I went into the bathroom late at night, there would be a dead woman in the bathtub. After *The Exorcist* I became convinced that the devil was living in our attic and reading old *National Geographics*, even though the rustling and thumping stopped after Mama caught a giant pack rat in a Havahart trap. Needless to say, I never take showers.

That's why I was shocked and appalled when Mama suggested we ride down to Tallahassee to see *The Silence of the Lambs*.

"You can't mean it!" I said. "We'll both be killed and skinned!"

"I won't be killed and skinned," she said smugly, "just you will be." She doesn't indulge these sick fancies of mine. We went to see *The Silence of the Lambs*.

There are times when you just don't want to sleep alone. I had two choices: First, I could creep through the house, my skin tingling and my eyes pressed wide against the dark, and sleep with Mama. But her blood-curdling snoring, with its gargling and squawking and its terrifying pauses is like the sound the devil might make if he were alternately relishing and strangling on a pound of human flesh.

Instead, I decided to sleep with my dog. My dog is very polite. He's more like a gentleman's gentleman in a collie dog suit. I begged him and begged him to jump up in bed with me—such a short little hop—but he just stood on the floor and gazed at me down that long, dignified nose of his. He has been trained not to get on the furniture. I ended up dragging my sheet and pillow down on his dog bed and curling up with him there, but he woke up and gave me a long look, then tiptoed on his prissy little feet to the corner, where he settled down with a sigh to sleep on the cold, bare floor.

I finally got my three goldfish and spent the night in the dog bed hugging the fishbowl and listening to something stalking around in the azalea bushes outside my room. Of course, the dog offers no protection: barking would disturb the peace of the night, and biting people would be downright rude.

But daylight is a wonderful tonic. I woke up the next day furry with dog hair, reeking of cedar, and feeling a little foolish. I didn't tell anyone about my night. My dog, of course, the very soul of discretion, will never mention it. It was just a movie, after all; there's nothing to be afraid of. Besides, Mama can catch anything in one of those Havahart traps.

Mama's Memoirs

For years we've been trying to get Mama to write her memoirs. She actually started once. She was writing them on old envelopes with a blue ballpoint pen. But she would make her grocery list on the other side of the envelope, and she kept leaving her memoirs at the checkout counter of Piggly Wiggly.

We bought Mama an electric typewriter, but the persistent hum made her nervous. "I can't stop and think with that humming," she said, glaring at the machine. "I feel like it's saying, 'Type, you old fool!'" Then my sister tried to train Mama to use a word processor. But she kept mashing the wrong buttons, and she ended up with three pages of dollar marks in her early childhood and a nine everywhere there should have been a space. And her account of the birth of her younger sister, Eleanor, turned out with every letter that should have been capital, small, and every letter that should have been small, capital—which, she said, gave a false sense of importance to the event.

"What I really need," she said, "is that old Underwood upright typewriter that used to sit under the sink." But my niece, Lucy, had taken that typewriter to college in Atlanta and had abandoned it when she got her first computer. So Mama had a good excuse not to write her memoirs.

Then, one summer, while cleaning out the attic of an old aunt in Saltville, Virginia, I found another Underwood upright typewriter. My aunt said I could have it, if I could just get it down from the attic and home on the train. The typewriter is the shape and size of a sperm whale. My aunt's husband, a newspaper journalist, had wrestled it up into the attic and then died. I rigged up a series of winches and pulleys and got it down.

Then I practiced different ways of carrying that typewriter. I'm strong for my size, so the sheer weight of it wasn't the problem. But if you tilt it the wrong way, the bell will ding and the carriage will swoop down and whack you in the knee. And I had to be fast and agile, because the train barely pauses at my station in Georgia. If you're not at the door with your bags and ready to leap off when the train begins to brake, you end up the next morning in Fort Lauderdale.

With the help of several gallant, old-fashioned uncles and a fluttering chorus of their wives making little shrieks and swapping yarns about hernias, I got the typewriter onto the train in Richmond. Then I was on my own. I staggered down the aisle to my assigned seat and plopped down beside a very alert looking young woman. "For my mother's memoirs," I gasped. The alert look changed to a kind of guarded disgust, and she clamped the headset of her portable tape player over her ears and began viciously reading a short story in her *New Yorker* magazine. I could barely hear the squeak of Beethoven's Fifth Symphony.

After a while I began to feel the flow of blood to my feet shut off, and I realized that I was going to have to get the typewriter off my lap and onto the overhead rack. I did it in two heaves, one to chest height, then up and onto the rack. At one point everything went black inside my head except for one bright light behind which I thought I could see my dead uncle, the journalist, dressed in white robes and beckoning earnestly to me across a deep valley. When I opened my eyes, my seatmate was gone. Only her *New Yorker* magazine was left, the pages still rustling. Later I heard her down the aisle, arguing with the attendant about assigned seats.

It was late at night when we got to Georgia. A

nice man from Ludowici had moved over to sit by me. "Your mama can type?" he asked.

"My mama can do anything," I said.

"Yeah," he said, "my mama is like that, too. But the one thing she can't do is type." He helped me get the typewriter off the train as it paused for its one instant.

We keep the typewriter on the kitchen table. Mama acts like she doesn't know it's there. But sometimes, late at night, I see a light on in the kitchen, and I hear a sound like somebody is out there cracking oysters open with a rock. And then I know Mama is writing her memoirs.

Memorizing Trollope

When she was a young girl, my cousin May had a morbid fear of cows. Her mother had died when May was just a little thing, and her crazy old father raised her. Cows didn't worry him, but he couldn't sleep at night for thinking up dreadful things that might happen to May. In the thin light of dawn these wild nighttime fantasies would distill themselves into precise, strict rules of conduct.

Poor May, still shuddering from the slobbery lips of the spavined cows of her nightmares, would bow her head over her cold cereal and meekly receive her father's orders: "You are not to swim in Reed's pond. And stay out of buildings with gas furnaces in the basement."

As May got older, the rules became less random and began to center around the perils of sexual maturity. Uncle Louis forbade her to speak on the telephone with any member of the opposite sex. Just the thought of the words of some randy young blade seeping into May's ear through those little holes in the earpiece made him shiver. And when he caught her reading *The Scarlet Letter*, he snatched the book from her and glued together all the pages that contained sexual references.

"It makes it hard to follow the story," May complained.

She began to spend a lot of time at our house. My mother made her welcome. One set of unnatural fears in a household is enough, she said. So May's father wrestled all alone in his big old house with his dark forebodings, and May slept in our spare room, moaning and tossing all night as the phantom cows slogged through her dreams.

"It's something about the way they put their feet down," she would explain to us in the morning. "And those lips—cow lips."

One night May had been trying on a dress Mama had made for her, and she was wearing only a slip when we heard Buck McCall come in the back door. May dashed out the front. It was a cold November night, and we thought she would hurry around the house, come in a side entrance, and get dressed. Buck stayed and stayed, but May did not reappear.

After he finally went home, we found her huddled in the yard, hugging her knees and shivering in her petticoat.

"There were cows," she chattered through blue lips, "cows at the door." Sure enough, two of our neighbor's cows had wandered into our yard. For almost an hour they had stood between May and the door, staring at her with their big cow eyes while she stood transfixed in her thin, white slip and stared back at them in the cold November moonlight.

The next morning May had a high fever, and she lay in bed sweating and raving about cows. Her father flew into the house with his eyes starting from their sockets. "It's that damned Buck McCall," he wailed. "She was out in the night with that damned Buck McCall!"

"No, Louis," my mother explained. "It was cows. She was out in the night with two cows."

"Cows!" Louis ranted. "That's impossible! She hates cows!"

There was no explaining things to Uncle Louis.

After a week May was better. She wouldn't talk, but she sat up in bed all day and all night and read Anthony Trollope. By the time she had finished the last volume, she was well.

But she was different. You could see it in her eyes. She had lost her fear of cows. And she could recite long passages of the Barsetshire novels from memory. We figured the high fever had permanently seared Trollope into her brain.

Uncle Louis came to get her. "May," he commanded, "you are not to stir from the house."

"Daddy," May said, "hush." She looked at him a long time with her new peaceful gaze. Uncle Louis didn't say another word. May drove him home.

After that day, May read anything she liked. She stayed out after dark. She even talked on the telephone with Buck McCall. But every night she and her father sat down in two rocking chairs and read Trollope out loud. Uncle Louis would read a chapter; then May would read. Of course, most of the time she didn't have to look at the page. The irrational proscriptions and the night cows were almost forgotten. And now, in talking about the past, we always refer to those troubled years delicately as "before May memorized Trollope."

Distillates

My aunt Eleanor thinks I should marry her nephew Kevin. The fact that Kevin has to lie down with a cold rag on his head after an hour in my company, and the fact that I can't seem to breathe normally when I am in the same room with Kevin, and have to go out on the porch and gulp air every ten minutes, does not signify to Aunt Eleanor.

"But your families are so close," she pleads.

"Our families are the same, Aunt Eleanor," I point out.

"A little inbreeding in a strong family is not a bad thing," she pronounces with a smack. Just the thought of inbreeding with Kevin takes my breath away, and I have to put my head down between my knees.

Kevin comes down from New York City for his annual visit to Aunt Eleanor every June. He wears all black clothes—black turtleneck shirt, tight black pants, and soft black suede boots. He comes to call on me. His mouth is set in a grim line, and sweat stands out on his face like clear fur. I turn the fan to blow on him, and we sit and drink iced tea with lemon. After a while I feel the need for air.

"Shall we take a short walk?" I ask.

"If you like," says Kevin.

We walk to the pond and back. On the way we talk about his main interest in life, which is a new form of dancing where the dancers hurl themselves at random around on the stage and scramble all over each other like mating frogs.

"It doesn't look to me like a whole lot of thought goes into it," I say. Kevin stiffens up and forgets to swing his arms.

On the way back from the pond we talk about my hobby, which is extracting the floral essences from certain aromatic plants using an alembic. I show him my storeroom full of green and brown bottles. I pop the tops off, and the fragrances drift through the room.

"That's lemon grass, that's rosemary, that's sacred basil," I tell him.

He sniffs each one delicately. Then he eyes the rows and rows of bottles, each neatly labeled with genus, species, and date. "But what's the point?" he asks.

Suddenly the air seems thin, and we go out on the porch. Kevin says good-night, I heave a sigh, and it's all over until his visit to Aunt Eleanor next June.

Finally the year comes when I just can't stand it again.

"Kevin," I ask, "do you want to marry me?"

Kevin's film of sweat breaks into trickles and runs off his chin. He looks at me hard, for the first time. "No!" he says. "Do you want to marry me?"

"Of course not," I say.

Kevin stretches out on the sofa. He pulls his shirttail out of his pants and wipes his face with it.

"I wonder why we keep doing this, year after year," I say.

"We do it because we both love Aunt Eleanor," Kevin says.

Now it's time for Kevin to go home, but he doesn't get up. He puts his feet up on the table and lays his arms across the back of the sofa. His feet in their black boots loll with the toes pointing out.

"Tell me how that thing works," he says, "that alembic."

I show him the water tank and the boiler. He takes the glass condenser and turns it gently in his hands. I explain how the water flowing through it cools the vapor products of distillation.

"And it drips out here," he says. "Show me."

I fill the beaker with chamomile leaves and assemble the machine. I fire it up. "The distillate will be blue," I tell Kevin, "because it's chamomile."

"Blue," he whispers.

He pulls up a chair and sits down. He arranges the flask to catch the drops and stares at the tip of the condenser.

I try not to laugh. "It takes a while, Kevin," I say.

But he keeps staring at the condenser until the first drop forms, quivers, and falls into the flask.

"See? It's blue," I say.

"Come here," Kevin says to me. "I'll show you something." He puts his hands on my waist. "Now jump up," he says. I jump as high as I can, and Kevin lifts me up across his shoulders. He leans over and we twirl around and around. I lay my head down, he pivots, and I slide down his back on my back. My feet are the last part of me to touch the floor. I can smell the chamomile as it drips faster and faster from the condenser. And I imagine that there is enough air in that room to float a hundred dancers on their toes.

Madness through Mirrors

I used to belong to the battery club at Radio Shack. I was wary at first. Every time I join any club, they make me be secretary. But the man at Radio Shack explained to me that there are absolutely no obligations in belonging to the battery club. All you have to do is walk into the store once a month and they give you a free battery, any size you want.

The other day when I went into Radio Shack for my free battery, there was a bank of television sets lined up at the entrance. They all showed the same picture—a woman opening a plate-glass door and walking into a big room. I felt like I had seen that woman before. Who is that woman? I asked myself. Who is that very familiar looking woman with those big old bony hands? It just so happened that the woman was me. It gave me such a turn that I left Radio Shack without my battery.

I had an ill-tempered old aunt Mathews whose descent into madness we traced through her own perception of her image in mirrors. Luckily this aunt never married and never had children, so the amount of damage she could do in the family was limited. Except for an occasional vicious little foray out among her nieces, she kept her meanness to herself.

The first sign we had that something was wrong came when she was in her seventies. She called the police and said that a strange woman was in her house. "She stares at me and yells at me. She's a mean old woman," my aunt told the police. They searched the house, but there was no sign of an intruder.

The next day my aunt called the police again. "She's back," she told them. This happened three times before the police gave up and called us.

My mother went over to my aunt's house to stay for a while. Late in the night she found my aunt standing in front of the mirror in the back bedroom. She was shaking all over and frothing at the mouth. "You ugly old woman," she growled hoarsely. "You bad, mean old woman. Get out. Get out of my house."

The next day Mama took the mirror down, and my aunt didn't call the police again.

My aunt got to where she didn't recognize some of us. And she would bite people with her mouth full of false teeth. We had to put her in a nursing home. Then a nurse called Mama. My aunt had been wandering around in the night until she found the mirror in the entrance hall. She would stand in front of it and talk.

"We don't know who she's talking to," the nurse said. She tried to remember what my aunt had said. "She said, 'You're no better than you ought to be, you young hussy.' Then she said, 'I saw you going out in the bushes with that black-headed Root Mc-Call down at Lake Sinclair. And you wearing that little shimmy-tail dress. You had your chance to do right, but you sure went wrong with your bad ways. You sure did go wrong.' "

The nurse asked our permission to lock my aunt into her room at night so she couldn't wander around and find the mirror, and we said that would be fine.

My aunt got very feeble. She didn't make sense when she talked. But when my niece, Lucy, finished up at Georgia Tech with a degree in physics, we thought the whole family should be there for her graduation. We put my aunt's wheelchair in the back of the car and drove up to Atlanta. I slept in the motel room with her to help her get to the bathroom at night.

Early in the morning when it was just beginning to be day, I woke up. My aunt was standing in front of the dresser. I had forgotten to cover up the mirror, and she was gazing into it. She had a look on her face I had never seen before. She leaned toward the mirror. She held one frail, trembling hand out to her reflection. And in the sweetest, quietest voice she said, "My name is Miss Mathews. And who are you, my dear little girl?"

I have had to give up my membership in the battery club. Living in the age of electronics as I do, I'm not afraid of mirrors. But I can easily imagine watching myself go crazy month by month on a whole bank of television sets at Radio Shack.

The Lips of a Stranger

We should have known things were not going well when Mama found a tick doing isometrics under her panty hose. Nothing along the tick's trudge up the evolutionary ladder had prepared him for panty hose, and he was exhausting himself scrambling and heaving against the nylon. Every now and then one of his knees would punch through the mesh. Mama and Louise and I were on our way to a cousin's wedding. It was a big wedding. She was marrying someone from "outside," and we had been told to look sharp.

"I've got to get him out of there," Mama said. "I have to go in from the top, and I can't do it sitting down. Besides, I've got to pull this panty hose up one more time before we go into church." Mama doesn't wear panty hose often, and she had bought queen size by mistake—she thought it meant the size of the average queen. The panty hose drooped around her legs in swags, and after she walked a few steps, the crotch would work its way down and appear below the hem of her dress, like a spectral pudendum. She started to pull off the road.

"You can't stop," my sister said. "We're late already." Nobody spoke. We were late because Louise had decided at the last minute that her knit dress made her look like a zipper. "It didn't look like this in the catalog!" she had wailed, eyeing herself sideways. Finally, after striking pose after pose in front of the mirror, she had discovered one rigid posture that was satisfactory, and with the fierce concentration of a tightrope walker she had maintained it since we left the house. Now she looked something like a ruler, the kind with the metal edge.

I was sitting in the backseat, admiring my lips in the rearview mirror. My cousin had given me some lipstick—not the ordinary kind but some beautiful iridescent goo in a little plastic tub with a screw-off top. Pot o' Gloss it was called; you rubbed it on with your finger. Now my lips looked and felt like the lips of someone I had never known. I had to keep them slightly parted, because when they touched, they were so slick they would skate across each other and leave little pearly smears of Pot o' Gloss all around the edges.

We came to the intersection of Highway 319 and

Butter and Egg Road. The cars on 319 were whizzing along, passing each other and honking their horns. Butter and Egg Road is dirt. Mama is a careful driver. She doesn't take risks. She always takes Butter and Egg Road.

"You're not going on Butter and Egg Road!" my sister commanded. "We'll get stuck. Look how muddy it is."

"Better to be stuck on Butter and Egg Road than killed on 319," Mama pronounced. "Besides, look at that set of tire tracks. Somebody made it through."

Louise allowed herself one huge sigh, then snatched herself upright again. We sloughed out onto Butter and Egg Road. The car skied and skewed, but Mama steered true. The red clay mud reminded me of Pot o' Gloss.

"None of these roads was paved when I was your age," Mama told us. "The secret is to steer with the skid."

I'd never understood what that meant. But I didn't care. I'd much rather just sit in the backseat studying my lips in the rearview mirror and let Mama drive. I'd seen lips like these in magazines, I decided, on women wearing billowy clothes who stalked along city streets in high-heeled shoes as if they knew where they were going and wanted to be going there.

"The lips of a stranger," I said out loud, watching them, as if by magic, form my words.

"I'm going to get Lyme disease from this tick," Mama said.

"Lyme disease hasn't gotten this far south yet," my sister gasped. The constraints of the rigid posture made speech difficult for her. "Besides, you can't stop now. We'd never get started again."

But soon we had to stop. The very truck whose tire tracks had been so encouraging at the entrance to Butter and Egg Road was stuck in the mud in front of us. We couldn't get around it.

"Oh no." Louise let out her air and slumped in the seat. "It's Ned Smalval." Ned Smalval had been sweet on her in a touching but infuriating way for years. He leaned in the window and looked us over.

"Whooo!" he said. "Look at y'all! Where are you going?"

"Let me out, Ned," said Mama. "We're going to a wedding, and I've got to get this tick out from under my panty hose."

"Look at that!" Ned marveled, eyeing the tick. "He's just a jumping and a jiving! That panty hose is mighty loose, though, don't you think, Mrs. White?"

"I accidently bought the wrong size," Mama said. "But if I keep it pulled up, it's not so bad."

"Gives the tick more scope, too, being that loose," Ned said.

He leaned up against our car, and we watched Mama head for the bushes, the crotch of her panty hose wagging between her knees. Ned took his hat off. "Kind of fetching, in a spooky sort of way," he mused.

My sister took her shoes off and stepped into the mud. She walked around and looked at the tires of Ned's truck.

"That's a real pretty dress, Louise," Ned called. "Pretty colors. Makes you look just like a zipper."

"Do you want us to help you push it, Ned?" I asked quickly.

"Nope. I'm going to get my daddy's tractor." And he loped off through the mud.

We waited.

"That Ned Smalval is a mighty nice boy," Mama announced.

"I'd rather be killed on 319," moaned Louise, slumping against the car door.

Ned came back with the tractor, slinging mud in all directions. We hooked up the chain to the bumper, and Mama steered while he pulled the truck to higher ground. Then we all four squeezed into the cab, and Ned took us to the wedding. Louise wiped the mud off her feet, put her shoes on, and sucked herself upright. Mama hiked up her panty hose one more time, and I checked the lips in Ned's side mirror. We were only a little bit late.

"Before you go in," Ned said to me, "you've got something all over your mouth." He rummaged under the seat and pulled out a filthy flannel rag. "Here's something to wipe it off with."

So much for Pot o' Gloss. So much for the lips of a

stranger. But, after all, I wondered, sitting in the pew between Mama and my sister, both elegantly serene in their queen-size panty hose and zipper knit dress, how would that magazine stranger with her high-heeled shoes and her shimmering lips fare on Butter and Egg Road the day after a heavy rain?

Zone 9

A Scourge of Swans

One day about ten years ago a fast-talking entrepreneur from New York moved into our neighborhood with a carload of brochures about exotic pets and an incubator the size of a Ford Bronco filled with swan eggs. We could all save our farms, send our children to college, and put new roofs on our houses with the extra income we would make by marketing swans. He would be our agent. We would raise the swans on our ponds, then he would buy them back from us and ship them up to fancy estates on the Hudson River where, he said, rich people would pay thousands of dollars to have a flock of swans to glide around in their reflecting pools.

"Fool Yankee," we said. But we tried it. Everyone

got four or five baby swans when the eggs hatched. Then, in the dark of night, the man from New York vanished, never to be seen again.

At first the natural elements took their toll on the swans. When they were still babies, the racoons and possums got a lot of them. In their gangly adolescence they were no match for the wild cats, and even after a year and a half, a big alligator could still swim under a swan, grab its black feet, and snatch it under water. But after three years nothing would touch those swans.

Every pond in our end of the county had at least a pair of them, gliding with an arrogant tranquility among the disgruntled alligators, who would open their jaws and hiss. The swans would turn their backs in graceful disdain, ruffle their feathers, and arrange their necks in a tighter S.

But the swans were vicious, selfish creatures. They chased the ducks out of the ponds and tore up the nests of the geese. The last straw came when a swan attacked Earl Castleberry's boat when he went out one summer afternoon to go fishing.

"Goddamn Yankee swan," Earl said. "I'm going to catch him and wring that scrawny neck."

"Just leave him alone, Earl," said Earl's wife. "Please just leave him alone."

"Can't even fish in my own pond," said Earl.

His friends tried to talk him out of it. They reminded him that even the alligators wouldn't touch the swans now.

"Hell," said Earl. "I ain't scared of nothing with feathers on it."

Earl did catch the swan that night. No one actually saw him do it, but we know that Earl dragged himself home from his pond, blinded in one eye, with a compound fracture of the wrist, and covered with deep cuts. After a week in the hospital he came home, a broken man. Now he lies out on his porch in the swing all day, and his friends sit in a semicircle around him with their elbows on their knees and their hands dangling between their legs.

"Let me take you fishing, Earl," one pleads. "I'll help you in and out of the boat."

"No," Earl says, shaking his head against the pillow, "no."

The fan ruffles his hair, and his friends look at the floor. Earl covers his good eye with a trembling hand. "It was the whiteness," he whispers. "It was the whiteness of him."

Earl's friends file out and stand around in the yard scuffing their feet and turning their backs to each other to sniffle. Sometimes they walk down to Earl's pond and stare at the swans. "Nothing," they say to each other, "nothing has a right to be that pretty."

At Earl's house there's talk of a nursing home. And on the ponds, slowly back and forth in elegant array, the swans parade.

Rattlesnake Belt

My mother and the octogenarian taxidermist down the road have a neat barter system going. Luther's worried about his loss of libido, and Mama loves hot peppers, so she trades him an aphrodisiacal herb from her garden, *Artemisia abrotanum* (a.k.a. Maiden's Ruin), for the jalapeño peppers he grows in his. She loves the peppers. He says he hasn't noticed any effect from the artemisia, except it seems to discourage moths.

"That's important to a taxidermist," she tells him. "At our age you take what you can get."

She also gives him dead rattlesnakes. He uses the skins to make rattlesnake belts. It's quite the fashionable thing where we live. He has other sources for the snakes, but he prefers hers because, he says, she doesn't kill them all over.

The snakes live under our house, and as long as they stay there, sedate and well behaved, Mama leaves them alone. But when they crawl out on warm spring mornings and spread themselves out in the sun on the back steps, it's a different story. "Hospitality can go just so far," says my mother, wielding her walking stick as she heads out to the back porch. Through the years she has perfected her technique. She sneaks the screen door open and carefully pins the snake's head against the bricks with a piece of firewood. Then she gives it one smart whack on the neck with the handle of her walking stick, and when the snake quits wiggling, she throws it in the back of her pick-up truck and drives it over to the taxidermist.

Every Saturday evening Luther and Mama get together and listen to "The Sounds of Swing" on the radio. She makes hot pepper vinegar and helps him lay sprigs of artemisia between his hides. He works on the belts, sewing the snakeskins to leather strips, punching holes, and inventing fancy buckles.

Last Saturday night a young man came to buy a custom-made belt. It had a sharp diamond pattern, beautifully centered, and the head cleverly concealed the buckle. Anyone could see how proud that boy was of that belt. Just strapping it on gave a new resonance to his voice and elasticity to his gait.

He swaggered out to his truck. It was one of those high-wheeled ones, with four-wheel drive and a loud radio, which he'd left playing. His girlfriend moved over to his side, and he drove off in a cloud of smoke and sound.

"That boy paid me $100 for that belt," said our neighbor, gazing after the truck.

"Jesus," said my mother, blinking in the vinegar fumes.

"Still," said our neighbor, turning back to "The Sounds of Swing" with a sigh, "it's a small price to pay for manhood."

County Fair

Every fall I go to the county fair. I stop first in the big metal building and look at the new agricultural machines, the monster tractors and combines with little glass houses on top where the modern farmer sits in air-conditioning and watches TV for acres and acres and acres. Big, dull-eyed men, with stooped shoulders and swagging bellies that keep a kind of syncopated time with their stride, gather around the tractors and stroke the tires that are higher than their heads.

Just outside the building a frail young man demonstrates an incredibly dainty rear-tine garden tiller, which he cranks with one feeble snatch of the cord and operates by strolling along beside the garden bed with two fingers on the handle. Although it only weighs twenty-five pounds, it digs to a depth of eight inches. "Your grandmother can operate this tiller," the young man tells his audience. "*Anyone* can operate this tiller." And with his thin, almost transparent skin and his weak-kneed gait and his pale, fluttering hands, he himself is living proof of that fact.

Out on the midway, slack-jawed women amble, their giant rumps packed into tight nylon pants like two shoats in a sack, and little stringy-haired children run around eating food made entirely of poisons. Hawkers with rotting snaggle teeth peddle dusty stuffed animals with polyester fur in shades of pink and purple just invented in this decade.

Finally I come to my favorite place at the county fair, the poultry barn. Great fans in the ceiling stir up the smells of sawdust and chicken feed. And down the middle of the long barn, in a double row of wire cages, are the prize-winning chickens. And what chickens they are!

These are the jewels of avian husbandry. Here are a brace of Sebright bantams—exquisite, alert little birds, with every golden feather overlapping its neighbor just so and edged in shimmering black. In the next cage is a Japanese silkie with no feathers at all, but instead, flowing tresses of down. Then a pair of Buff Cochins, in softest tan and all puffed up, with smooth, rounded rumps and feathery feet. There are the game roosters strutting in their cages, their chests thrown out, their gracefully arched tail feathers an iridescent black shading into indigo and violet, their spurs clicking as they turn.

At the end of the row is a cage of parti-colored Auracanas from South America, also called Easter egg chickens. In a wire rack below their cage are the eggs they have laid that day. One egg is the palest green, one is a rosy pink, one is the blue of the October sky. The barn is filled with the gentle cooing and soft growling of chickens at peace. The light is dim. The air is cool.

But soon it's time to leave the poultry barn. It's almost dark and the rides have started. People are milling around the concession tents in great flocks. There's that unmistakable smell of humans in the subtropics. A woman squats down and feeds her baby something bright red on a stick. Another mother smacks her little girl on the side of the head because she's whining. My fellowmen.

Riding home from the fair, I think how strange and wonderful, how much flash and strut and style, and what shades of blue and green and buff there would be if all humans were banished from this earth, and the world were peopled entirely by prize-winning chickens.

Flying Saucer

My mother is old, but she doesn't make up stories that aren't true, and she doesn't see things that aren't there. That's why we didn't doubt her for a minute when she told us she had seen a flying saucer go over the house early one spring morning.

She was lying in her bed on the screen porch when she saw it coming down. She unlatched the door and went out into the yard for a better look. It was round, flat, silent, and surrounded by yellow flames. It hovered over the garden for a minute. Then, without a sound, it was gone. Our dog, who is not the excitable type, barked wildly and ran around and around.

Mama called the young man down the road, who is crazed on the subject of extraterrestrial life.

Within an hour the yard was swarming with UFO enthusiasts. One of them set to work with calipers to measure the little cone-shaped holes the armadillos had dug all over the yard during the night. Another took samples of grass, leaves, and dirt and put them into carefully labeled plastic bags.

Our wild-eyed neighbor, Darrell, interviewed Mama. His bristly red hair was standing on end. "Exactly when . . . ? How long . . . ? What color? What shape? How big?" He eyed our dog. "Does your dog always sleep that much?"

"Well, he's old. He sleeps a lot." Mama said defensively.

But Darrell explained that sometimes after an encounter of this kind, pets will exhibit strange behaviors. "And yourself," he continued, "did you notice any unusual depression, dullness of mind, or euphoria after the sighting?"

"No," said Mama, "I'm pretty steady, for a person my age."

"And these red spots on your arm?"

"Ant bites."

"Did you lose any time?" He told us that sometimes these spaceships take humans on board. They keep them for a few hours, performing fiendish experiments on them, taking tissue samples, and probing all their orifices with nimble fingers. Then they return the humans home. Because of the strange hypnotic state induced by the spacemen, the people have no recollection of the experience. Only their clocks tell them that hours have passed. It's called "lost time."

"Nope, no lost time," Mama told him. "My coffee was still hot."

"How about this brown area, right under where the saucer descended? The grass everywhere else is green."

"That's our cover crop this year—brown-topped millet."

The UFO people sighed. Our neighbor's hair seemed calmer than when he first arrived. Mama felt that she had disappointed them. They got into their cars and drove away.

But since that day Mama has read everything she can get her hands on dealing with UFOs and extra-terrestrial life. I, not being as thorough a scholar as she, just skim for the best parts: the pointy-headed creatures that creep and creep through your house at night and stare at you with their almond eyes as you sleep, and the dreaded "men in black" who cleverly insinuate themselves into your company and ask questions. They're really not men, of course, and they wear the black clothes to disguise the fact that there's nothing inside.

A man did come into the yard one day in July, but he was wearing plaid Bermuda shorts and said he was a census taker. "Still," Mama said ominously, "you can never tell what concessions the men in black might have to make for a south Georgia summer day."

Campaign Promises

A few years ago my mother got interested in politics. A very fine man named Vernon Bryan was running for a high political office in our region. There was only one problem: this is south Georgia and Vernon Bryan is black. I don't know how Mama got so wise without getting any smarter, but she was sure he would win.

"What do you mean he can't win?" she asked. "He's the best man for the job." And she licked a stamp and mailed off another social security check to his campaign fund.

As election time grew closer, she worked harder and harder. She drove her old pickup truck into town every day to man campaign headquarters, and she spent hours studying voter registration lists and calling on the phone to urge people to vote. She volunteered for everything. The campaign manager for our area took me aside. "You've got to talk your mama out of driving people on election day," he said. "They'd never get to the polls with your mama driving."

She was most useful, though, at parades, rallies, and fund-raising events with news coverage. Surveys had shown that Mr. Bryan did not have the support of elderly rural white women. So after every speech, he would scan his audience, searching for Mama's face. Then he would climb down and make his way through the crowd to shake her hand while the cameras whirred. She was careful to wear a different dress to every event, so no one could tell it was the same old white woman every time.

Mr. Bryan fell lower and lower in the polls. Mama sat up at the deserted campaign headquarters, reading *Parting the Waters* and packing bumper stickers into boxes to mail back to Atlanta. We drove all the way to a park in Albany, Georgia, for one last rally. Everybody knew by then that it was all over, but they must have decided not to let it keep them from having a good time.

We could smell the barbeque and hear the rap music before we even got to the city limits. Both sides of the road were lined with cars, and we had to drive almost a mile away from the pavilion where Mr. Bryan was making his speech before we found a place to park.

It was August, and Mama slowly and feebly made her way back up the road, tapping her walking stick on the smoking asphalt. She was wearing her last different dress, white with little sprigs of flowers. By the time we got to the park entrance, it was drenched with sweat. People made way for her, and someone brought her an aluminum chair, a Styrofoam cup of lukewarm water, and one of those fans they give out at funerals.

Mr. Bryan finished his speech and came over to us. His voice was hoarse and his smile was weary. I could tell his feet were aching. "Let's shake hands one last time for these cameras," he said to Mama. She wiped the sweat off her face and smiled. They shook hands. Shutters clicked. Mr. Bryan winced. Then he sat down and rested his elbows on his knees.

"This is not the last time we will shake hands, sir," Mama said to him. "I will be there to shake your hand when you become president of the United States."

Mr. Bryan made sure the cameras were loaded back into the big white vans before he leaned over and gave her a tiny kiss on the cheek. "I know you will be there, Mrs. White," he said.

Leave-taking

Every summer I take a three-week vacation up north. I look forward to it all year. About a week before I leave, I start getting ready. I pack my bag, I buy a box of raisins to eat on the train, and I get down all the good books I haven't had time to read all year. I mow the lawns around the house. I clean out the freezer. I weed the garden. I wash my dog. I put everything in its place. I make Mama sit out in the yard for a day while I mop all the floors in the house. I even launder the curtains and the slip-covers on the furniture.

I prepare little packages of food for Mama to eat while I'm gone, mostly bean and rice and grain dishes. I've been on a year-long campaign to reform her bad eating habits. She peers into the freezer at the neatly labeled packages.

"No ice cream?" she asks plaintively.

"Cholesterol," I snap. "And remember: Buddy gets only two cups of dry dog food and a heartworm pill each day."

"No cookie bones?" Mama asks.

"There's no nutrition in those cookie bones," I say. I'm a good daughter and a responsible pet owner.

Finally there's only one day before I leave. And that's when the horrible pangs of homesickness begin. I walk around the neat and tidy rooms of my house and smell the fresh-bleached fabrics and the Murphy Oil Soap and look out the gleaming windows over the beautiful lawn that still retains the mower stripes. "I don't want to leave," I cry.

I wake my dog up and hug him and hug him. He has a clean, citrusy flea-soap smell. "I'm leaving you, Buddy," I sob into his fur. He rolls his eyes. "I may be killed and never return. The train may derail. I could be murdered in Pennsylvania Station. You may never see me again."

He flops back down and sighs. He's not one of these wonderfully intuitive dogs who amazingly sense that their masters are leaving and then mope and pine and hover near and look on with soulful eyes. In spite of the fact that I've been parading around with my knapsack on my back, practicing my travel gait, and making phone calls to 1-800-USA-RAIL for over a week, he doesn't seem to have a clue.

That last night, I sit up in bed feeling so maudlin and nostalgic that I eat up my whole box of travel raisins and read most of the books I'd packed, just to comfort myself. I go for a last stroll in the moonlight to think my melancholy thoughts. But before I get out of the yard, I step on a frog in the dark and squash him and have to go back in the house. It doesn't seem like a good omen.

In the morning Mama takes me to the train station. Buddy sleeps in the backseat. He barely looks up as I unload my bags. I fight back the tears and hug Mama good-bye. I wave from the train window. She waves back. Buddy stands up in the backseat and looks after the train as it pulls out of the station.

Mama smiles—but it's not a wan and wistful smile. It's more like a grin. As the train chugs down the track, that grin spreads over her whole face. And in the backseat, Buddy wildly wags his tail.

An Interesting Life

Sometimes I go to visit my old friend Mrs. Bierce. We drink lemonade out of amazingly thin crystal glasses with inaccessible filigree handles. The gold wash on the rim has long ago been worn away by the application of many gentle lips. A maid passes cheese wafers on a tiny silver dish. I could eat the whole plateful, but I know to take only one. It is the hospitality of another age.

Mrs. Bierce, transformed by the years into a pile of lumps, sits back in her easy chair. I teeter on the edge of a Queen Anne side chair, and we converse. Mrs. Bierce wears thick bifocal lenses, and her eyes loom as big as litchi nuts behind the glass. One eye has a tendency to wander, and just when I think I have a bead on it, off it goes.

At first the stilted gentility and the wandering eye made conversation halting, but Mrs. Bierce has led an interesting life, and after the first few visits she had my complete attention.

One day she showed me a small painting done all in dashes and streaks of unlikely colors. At one edge of the frame sat a sullen, very handsome man frowning out of the shadows. At the other edge, heading out of the picture with a toss of her elegant head and a twinkle in her merry eyes went a beautiful woman, all in shades of aqua and pink. "My husband and me," Mrs. Bierce explained. I took it to be a portrait of her marriage.

On my last visit Mrs. Bierce told me the story of her education. Her parents thought every child should learn at least three languages, and their plan was to send her to a different country every year for her schooling. It was 1912, and the First World War aborted their plans. To this day Mrs. Bierce speaks only English.

They did make a start, though, and in the spring of 1912, at age eight, she was put on a ship bound for Germany for her first year of schooling. Even at that age she must have exhibited the charm so evident in the portrait I had seen of her as a young woman, because she told me that the captain of the ship took her on as a sort of adoptive granddaughter during their passage. She followed him around all day and even took her meals with him in his cabin.

One night a steward woke her up and told her

the captain wanted her to come to the bridge at once. He had something he wanted to show her. She hurried up and stood by him at the rail.

"And there," she told me, "we saw the most exciting thing one can see while on board a ship at sea—another ship!" The night was dark, and the only sound was the lapping of the waves. Mrs. Bierce says she doesn't remember whether it was warm or cold—only the sight of that magnificent ship, lit up from bow to stern, silently gliding past in the night. The silence, the blackness of the water, and the remoteness of the passing ship made her think of great depth and the mysteries of things she did not know. The captain's voice startled her when he finally spoke.

"Take a good look, my child," he told her. "You are seeing history in the making, for that ship is no ordinary one, but the greatest ship ever built. It is the RMS *Titanic* on her maiden voyage."

The ice tinkles in our glasses. I don't eat the last cheese wafer. Mrs. Bierce's eye wanders off somewhere. It certainly has been an interesting life.

Semen and Daffodils

It's so easy to fall in love on a train. There's something romantic about hurtling through the night, not knowing what state you're in. It makes your blood flow sluggish.

It happened to me on a trip to Boston, Massachusetts. I was taking a sack of daffodil bulbs to my uncle, who missed the daffodils of his childhood home. It was an overnight train ride. I was wearing a maternity dress. I wasn't pregnant, but I had to change train stations in New York City. New York City scares me, and I had a theory that people would treat me sweetly and not hit me over the head and steal the daffodils if they thought I was pregnant.

Then somewhere in north Georgia, or it could have been South Carolina, I fell in love with the man in the seat beside me. He had a wonderful smile and was very kind. He began telling me about his work, which was the artificial insemination business. He traveled all over the world studying bulls and collecting their semen for the American Breeders' Association.

After a while he reached under his seat and took out a leather briefcase and unfastened the clasps. I shut my eyes and held my breath, but instead, the briefcase was neatly filled with pamphlets in full color showing famous bulls, beautifully posed, and listing rows and rows of statistics about the milk production of their offspring.

I had a little Jersey cow myself at the time, and we talked all night long about travel and cows and the American Breeders' Association—and daffodils. The moon was full, and we could see the country drifting by our window, the shacky little railroad towns, the flowery meadows, with Queen Anne's lace like floating silver coins, and herds of cows with the moon shining on their flanks. Then at dawn, the monuments in Washington.

When we finally got to Pennsylvania Station in New York City, I shook his hand and said good-bye. But he wouldn't let me go. "How are you going to get this fifty pounds of daffodil bulbs across town to Grand Central?" he asked.

I didn't understand. "Carry them," I said.

"You shouldn't be carrying heavy things," he said. And he grabbed up my bag of bulbs and headed across Times Square. I followed behind him trying to figure it out. Why shouldn't I carry heavy things?

It was only after he had settled me and the bulbs on the train to Boston and strode off on his search for the perfect bull that I remembered. With all the talk about semen and daffodils I had completely forgotten about pretending to be pregnant. And that whole night, when I had been thinking of him in ways that don't bear mentioning, he had been thinking of me as a foolish little pregnant woman risking the life of her unborn child to transport fifty pounds of daffodil bulbs halfway across a continent to a homesick old uncle in Boston.

It was frustrating. When I got home, instead of dragging my cow by the horns down the road to my neighbor's bull as I had done in the past, I just called the local agent of the American Breeders' Association. The next day he came out wearing a long rubber glove and a bowler hat.

And nine months later, on a moonlit night with the daffodils in full bloom, I delivered my cow of a fine little Jersey heifer.

Teaching Luther to Cook

Early in the summer our neighbor, an old taxidermist named Luther, came into our house with two jars. He had been trying to cook, and he wanted some advice. My mother and I are both good cooks. We have those cool pastry hands, fine-tuned noses, and an understanding of sauces. We sat down at the kitchen table, and Luther opened his jars.

"I want to ask you if you think these pickles are too limp and this blackberry jam is too sweet."

He fished around in the jar and pulled out a pickle. It lay across his fingers like a giant tadpole. Biting into that pickle was like eating a sour oyster with a thin green skin. I scraped it off my hands back into the jar. "Jesus, Luther, do you have to ask?" I said.

Mama gave me a look, chewed silently, and said, "Luther, the flavor is very good."

"Who cares about the flavor with a pickle like that?" I asked.

Luther sighed and opened the blackberry jam. We each got a spoon and dipped in. Luther watched us anxiously. I tasted it. I could feel the enamel beginning to slide off my teeth. I rushed over to the sink and washed out my mouth.

Mama cut a slice of bread and spread blackberry jam all over it. She ate the whole thing. Beads of sweat broke out on her forehead.

"It is a little sweet, Luther," she said, holding the jar up to the sunlight, "but it's got a lovely color." I could see sugar crystals forming on the glass.

I screwed the tops tightly back on the jars. Luther slumped in his chair disconsolately and stared down into his lap.

"Luther," Mama said, with a lilt in her voice. I put my head in my hands. I had heard that lilt before. It is the first sign that Mama is about to tackle an impossible project, something like teaching a fish to sing or a cow to dance the schottische.

"Luther," she said, "cooking is not like tanning hides." It was her first lesson in teaching Luther how to cook.

We watched him shuffle back up the road home with his pickles and his jam. I went to brush my teeth. Mama gave me a good scolding. "How could you say those mean things to that poor man?" she asked. "Did you see that pitiful look in his eyes? He'll probably never try to cook anything again in his life."

"Hallelujah," I said. I think it was the pickle that made me feel so mean.

"And here you are," said Mama, "a professional first-grade schoolteacher, talking like that. All he needs is a little encouragement and instruction."

"All right," I warned, "but remember when you tried to teach that jaybird to fly—that jaybird with one wing shot off."

"That bird did very well," Mama snapped. And she flounced off to the kitchen to gather up her tools to take to Luther's house for his first session.

They started with Jams and Jellies. Mama gently taught him that blackberries are to jelly cooks what polyester leopard-skin-print fabric is to taxidermists. The very finest jelly, the chinchilla of jellies, comes from mayhaws.

Mayhaws are fiendishly tiny, bright red, achingly tart berries that grow wild in Southern swamps. You gather them by wading in waist-deep black water and scooping them up with a net. Alligators float by, giving you their sidelong glances, and then disappear with a wink, and fat cottonmouth moccasins slither off the muddy banks.

Mama and Luther spent one whole Saturday in the swamp gathering mayhaws. Mama came in late at night covered with mosquito bites, but happy. Luther had made three jars of mayhaw jelly under her supervision.

"Tart?" I asked.

"It took some doing to get him off that bag of sugar, but yes, that jelly will make your mumps sit up and sing," she said. She rubbed calamine lotion on her bites and crawled into bed.

"This is all very good," I said. "I just hope you don't die of malaria, teaching Luther to cook."

They went on to Pickles and Preserves. Mama came home after the first lesson very discouraged. She put one hand on my arm and the other over her mouth. Her eyes were wide with horror. "He was *cooking* those cucumbers," she whispered.

But after a week of work she was satisfied. She brought me a jar of bread-and-butter pickles to sample. "Luther made these all by himself," she said with pride. I had to admit they were pretty good—not too sweet, with a good mustardy bite. "He's developing a nice sense of proportion," Mama said.

Biscuits and Pastry was hard on her, though. Day after day she came home shaking her head. "A heavy hand," she sighed, "a heavy, heavy hand."

But he made up for it when they started Bread Making. "You should see that man knead," Mama said, picking flour out of her ears. "He says it's a technique he learned in the tanning vats."

By the end of July they had been through Sauces and Marinades, Shellfish, and Game. At the beginning of August I went on my vacation. I sent Mama postcards from Virginia Beach and Cape May, New Jersey. "Wish you were here!" they said.

She sent me one letter: "Some difficulty with Soufflés. On to Desserts this week. See you soon."

When I got back, it was almost time for my school to begin. And Luther had completed his course. Mama had that peaceful, satisfied look of a person who has done well and knows it. They had planned a graduation dinner. Luther was preparing it all by himself. Of course, I wasn't invited.

About 6:00 P.M. Mama put on her white dress with the little sprigs of flowers. I helped her button it up in the back and watched her head up the road. "I hope you don't come home with ptomaine poisoning!" I called after her.

The house was still. Summer was almost over. I had a restless, uneasy feeling—a mixture of regret, shame, and sour grapes. I heated a can of soup and ate it at the kitchen table. I hadn't stirred it enough, and I kept coming up on cold lumps. I tried to read, but I couldn't keep my mind on my book.

Finally I went out in the backyard. It was dusk. I looked through the woods toward Luther's house and imagined the magnificent loaf of yeast bread with its crusty shoulders, the curried chicken, the twang of ginger in the mango chutney, and the rosy glow of the mayhaw jelly with its faintly floral note. And I swear I could almost hear those pickles snap.

Buzzard

There was something in the road. I drove closer to it. It was a buzzard eating a dead armadillo. I got closer. It was a big buzzard. And I'd never seen a buzzard's tail feathers so bleached and pale.

That buzzard better move, I thought. I'd never had to slow down for a buzzard before. They always lope out of the way. I got closer.

The buzzard turned his head and looked at me. He stood up on his big yellow legs. His head was snow white. His eyes were gold. He wasn't a buzzard. He was a bald eagle.

Then, not until after I had brought the car to a full stop, he spread his wings and with a slow swoop lifted himself into the air. He turned his head and

156

gave me a long look through the car windshield with his level yellow eyes. Then he slowly wheeled up into the sky until he was just a black dot against the blue.

I turned the car off. I thought about that glare he had given me: What are *you* doing here? it had said. When I got started again, I drove slower and felt smaller. I think it does us all good to get looked at like that now and then by a wild animal.

Homecoming

I just got back from my vacation. I went to Washington, New Hampshire, for two weeks. Mama was glad to have me back. I had asked my sister, Louise, and my uncles Jimbuddy and Sonny to look in on her now and then while I was gone, and they had been pestering her with their attentions. My sister had dragged her to the movies to see Madonna. "You just sit here and stagnate all day long," my sister had told her. "You need to get out more, see what's going on in the world."

So Mama saw Madonna. It worried her. "What if you had turned out like that?" she said to me. And Jimbuddy spent every afternoon with her. He ate two gallons of chocolate ice cream while I was gone,

Mama told me. All in all, she prefers my method of caretaking—benign abuse and neglect.

"By the way," she said as I unpacked my bags, "a big white oak snake moved into your room while you were gone. I started to put him out," she said, "but he gave me that look."

"That cool look," I said.

"That's right," she said.

We have had a little problem with mice in the house, and Mama prefers snakes to cats as mousers. Snakes are silent, they don't trip you up rubbing against your legs, and they don't shed hair.

The snake is living in our Christmas decorations on the fireplace mantel. We put up balsam boughs from Maine at Christmastime, and we don't take them down until the following November because it's only when the balsam gets really dry, about July, that it has its sweetest smell.

I don't have an unnatural fear of snakes, as some people do, but I'm not sure I like the idea of having one living in the same room with me. "What if he crawls up the bedpost in the dark of night and creeps between the sheets with me?" I ask Mama.

"These hot summer nights," she says reassuringly, "you'll just be grateful for the coolness of him."

Gardening

About six years ago, like so many romantic gardening fools, I fell for it: the wildflower meadow. I don't know whether it was the pictures on the seed packets, or the vision I had of myself, dressed all in white, strolling through an endless vista of poppies and daisies.

"A garden in a can," the seed catalogs said. The pictures showed a scene of rolling hills and dales, an area about the size of Georgia and Alabama combined, covered solid as far as the eye could see with billowing drifts of lupine and phlox.

But I wasn't born yesterday. I had been tricked by those pictures before. I come from down south, where vegetation does not know its place. Honeysuckle can work through cracks in your walls and strangle you while you sleep. Kudzu can completely shroud a house and a car parked in the yard in one growing season. Wisteria can lift a building off its foundation, and certain terrifying mints spread so rapidly that just the thought of them on a summer night can make your hair stand on end.

I knew what Lady Bird Johnson was talking about when she gave the wildflower romantics a look and said, "You can't just scatter the seeds around as if you were feeding chickens." Even the more responsible plant catalogs, in their offer of wildflower seed mixes for the various regions of the country admitted, "We have not been able to develop a mixture suitable for Zone 9." So I knew it wouldn't be easy.

But it's hard to squash a romantic. I made a plan. I would prepare my ground, about a half acre, and plant the wildflowers in rows. I would keep the weeds out for five years, by cultivating between the rows with a push plow and a hoe, and weeding by hand within each row. By the end of those five years, I figured I would have eliminated any perennial weeds and weed seeds. Then the garden would be on its own. The wildflowers would spread, eventually taking up the spaces between the rows, and I would get out my white dress and begin my leisurely strolls.

My garden's first spring: the seeds arrived. I planted by hand. The rows, neatly set out with stakes and string, seemed endless. I crawled up and down and up and down every afternoon examining each seedling as it sprouted. Was this spotted spurge or sweet Annie? Red-root pigweed or showy primrose? I recognized most of our common weeds and tweaked them out.

After every rain I hoed between the rows. My hands got hard and callused. They took on the curve of the hoe handle so that everywhere I went, I looked as if I were gripping a ghostly hoe.

The first summer, my annual plants bloomed. The *Coreopsis tinctoria* was spectacular, a glowing red, and the cosmos was shoulder high. Its lavender petals brushed my face as I scritched and scritched up and down each row. I loved the sight of the clean brown earth stretching away from the blade of my hoe. On my hands and knees I weeded between plants. My knees ached, but the smell down there was nice, damp ground and bruised artemisia. I developed a gardener's stoop and a horticulturist's squint.

That first winter, I could relax only a little. Bermuda grass can establish itself during a winter and get away from you the following spring. So every evening at dusk, I would stalk up and down my garden like a demented wraith, peering at the ground for each loathed blue-green blade, my cloak billowing in the wind and my scarf snagging on the bare gray branches of last summer's sunflowers.

At night, I would lie in my bed under the quilt listening to the wind outside and pinching and sniffing the little bunches of sweet Annie I had harvested and dried in July. I dreamed of that summer, only four years away now, when the garden would be finished. My white dress would be linen, I decided.

The second summer was very fine. Some of the annuals had reseeded, and the perennials and biennials bloomed for the first time. But I had a real problem with something called Old Horrible Snakeroot, one of the terrifying mints, creeping in around the edges. Every afternoon, dressed in a wide straw hat, big boots, and little else, and pouring sweat, I violently hoed the perimeter of my garden. I wore out my first hoe that year with sharpening the blade, and the handles of my Little Gem cultivator became as smooth as ivory.

During the third and fourth years the rows began to close in. There were great irregular patches of gaillardia spanning several rows, with Queen Anne's lace and moss verbena weaving themselves among clumps of black-eyed Susans. When I stood up to ease my back and looked across the garden, I could see that it was truly as beautiful as the picture in the Park's seed catalog. I wiped the sweat out of my eyes and washed my face in the watering can. My white linen dress would have lace.

The fifth summer, I had to go to the doctor about my knees. "You've got to quit squatting down," he told me.

"I can't quit squatting down," I said. "I've got a

garden." He sighed and gave me a pair of elastic bandages.

I had a problem with thistles that year. The seeds must have blown in from somewhere. I wore gloves to pull them out, and every time I took out a thistle, I would transplant a wildflower in its place. Every one of the transplants thrived and multiplied, and by the end of that summer, there was not a spot of bare ground for a weed seed to settle in. My garden was complete.

That winter I bought the linen and the lace and sewed my white dress.

In March I went out to the garden. The linaria was the first thing to bloom. I knew it would be. I knew that a week later the verbena would show up, then the shasta daisies and the gaillardia—a clump here, here, and here. In midsummer the Queen Anne's lace would begin to bloom. I knew exactly how it would be. I knew the name of every plant. I could recognize each one even before it got its true leaves.

I sighted down the length of the garden. There was no trace of the neat rows I had worked and worked for all those years. The garden had taken over itself, just as I had planned.

I walked back to the house. I looked at my soft, limp hands. I looked at my white linen dress, with lace. It seemed like the stupidest thing I had ever thought up. "The fact is," I said to myself, "I want something to hoe."

I've started reading about intensive gardening. It involves double digging and raised beds. Every season you pull out the old plants and put in new ones. It's a garden that never gets finished.

I gave the white dress to my sister, Louise. Sometimes she comes for a visit and strolls in the wildflower meadow. She ooohs and aaahs and brings her friends to see it. They pick armloads of flowers. I sit on the edge and draw diagrams of my next season's garden in the raised beds. I'm learning about companion planting.

In the wildflower meadow, the Queen Anne's lace waves its filigree heads over the marsh pinks, and the sweet alyssum tucks up neatly around the clumps of painted daisies. But I hardly notice. I've got a new garden now.

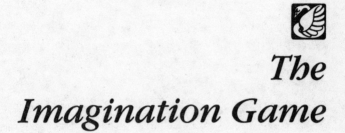

The
Imagination Game

Maritime Disasters

I've been teaching children to read for fifteen years now. I've seen the teaching methods come and go. When I first started teaching first grade, we used the word-list method. Children would memorize lists of words, and when they knew enough words, say ten or twelve, they could read little stories composed of those words. Believe me, those were some dreary stories. It was hard to keep the children's interest.

So we went on to the cute-idea teaching method. A teacher would make construction paper teddy bears whose arms and legs could be attached by matching a contraction to its long form, or dogs who could reach their food bowls by displaying the correct beginning consonant through holes in their heads. Other teachers would say, "What a cute idea!" Then they would make construction paper teddy bears and dogs and dog bowls. Some children learned to read; some didn't. And at the end of the day, with my classroom strewn with dismembered teddy bears and starving construction paper dogs whose bowls were permanently lost, I would think, There must be a better way.

Then a few years ago I found it: maritime disasters. Give me a man overboard or a good sinking ship, and I can teach a half-witted gorilla to read. I start with old sea chanties. The children rub their fingers under the written words on their song sheets as the singers on the tape recorder yowl out the tales at a dirgelike pace—exactly the speed beginning first-graders read.

> So his messmates pulled him up,
> but on the deck he died.
> And they stitched him in the hammock
> which was so fair and wide.
> And they lowered him overboard,
> but he drifted with the tide,
> and he sank into the Lowland, Lowland, low,
> he sank into the Lowland Sea.

When children get the idea that written words can tell them something absolutely horrible, half the battle of teaching reading is won.

And that's when I turn to the *Titanic*. The children sit on the rug at my feet, and I tell them the story. It's almost scary to have the absolute, complete attention of that many young minds.

I bought a little cardboard model of the ship and spent a week and a half folding down flaps and inserting tabs to assemble it.

I used up three years' worth of bonus points from the Lucky Book Club to buy a classroom set of Robert Ballard's book *Exploring the* Titanic: *How the Greatest Ship Ever Lost Was Found*. It's written on a fourth-grade reading level—lots of hard words—so I tipped in pages with the story rewritten on an easier level. But by the end of the second week the children are clawing up my pages to get at the original text underneath.

Little boys who couldn't pass the Draw a Man test in September are now turning out recognizable portraits of Captain Smith and Robert Ballard in eight colors with their blunt-tipped first-grade crayons, and Styrofoam cups and paper clips are transformed into models of Ballard's underwater remote-controlled robot. The children learn to read, and I haven't had a cute idea in years.

Sometimes I still worry though. Robert Ballard, who first found the *Titanic* more than seventy years after the disaster, deplores the pilfering and artifact gathering of subsequent explorations of the wreck. He thinks it's like desecrating a grave. And some afternoons when the children are gone home, I sit all alone in my empty classroom surrounded by sketches of a wall-eyed Captain Smith and wonder if my use of the *Titanic* is not just as exploitative.

Then I remind myself that in my whole career the *Titanic* and I will teach over a thousand children how to read—close to the number of people who lost their lives on that black night. Surely, for the sake of literacy, the spirits of those poor souls will forgive me.

Grandparents' Day

I dreaded Grandparents' Day last year. It was our principal's idea. All the grandparents of our students were invited to drink coffee in the lunchroom, and then go to their grandchildren's classrooms to sit in on a lesson. I hate to teach school in front of grownups. And grandparents would be the worst. Children don't behave the way many members of that generation think they should. They don't always say, "Yes, Ma'am," and, "No, Ma'am." What if a child said something to shock the grandparents? What if I did?

The grandparents filed in and sat in a row of chairs facing the children. I plodded on with my regular lesson about the sinking of the *Titanic*. I was explaining how the iceberg buckled the metal plates on the side of the ship. After a while I got that feeling so familiar to first-grade teachers that no-body was listening to me. I looked around.

There at the blackboard with a piece of chalk in his knobby fist stood Johnny Mason's old grand-father. He was drawing the *Titanic*. He scribbled and cross-hatched vigorously, and then, through the chalk dust, the split seam appeared like a piece of folk art *trompe l'oeil*. With his hands he showed the gap. A little boy turned to me. "So that's what you were trying to say," he said.

That afternoon I called Mr. Mason on the tele-phone. We talked about the *Titanic*. It seems that he had been interested in the ship his whole life. He had read every book and article that had ever been written on the subject.

I knew it was a big favor to ask. But I had a feeling it would be worth it. "Would you . . . ? Would it be too much . . . ?"

But "Yes," said Mr. Mason, "I'll come. I'll be glad to come." He would give his talk in the auditorium, he said, because he would need the stage. And he would need his grandson Johnny to assist him. He thought a while. "Give me a week," he said.

And a week later, at 10:00 A.M., we assembled in the auditorium. Mr. Mason was standing on the stage in front of the closed curtains. "I'm a little nervous," he whispered to me. His shoes were shined, his shirt was starched, and his hair retained the marks of the comb teeth. Under the curtain we could see the attentive and expectant feet of his grandson.

He began at the shipyard in Belfast. He was a little shaky at first, but he knew his audience. He knew better than to lose them with a recital of statistics in tons and feet: " . . . as long as from the rose bed in front of the schoolhouse to the library downtown," he explained. And, "One of those propellers wouldn't fit in your classroom. It might just fit in this auditorium." Eyes rolled up to the ceiling and down the walls. A sound rose and fell like the tide—the sound of thirty first-graders whispering "Wow."

Mr. Mason has a low, growly voice and is absolute master of the dramatic pause. By the time he got to the launching of the ship on May 31, 1911, he had found his pace, and the children were straining forward in their seats with their eyes and mouths wide open. And then Mr. Mason cleared his throat conspicuously. It was a cue.

Under the curtain we saw his grandson's feet spring into action. We heard the creak of pulleys, the red curtains parted, and there on the stage was revealed a twenty-foot model of the *Titanic* in plywood and Styrofoam. If Captain Smith himself had been raised from his watery grave and seated before them in his gleaming white-and-gold uniform, the children could not have been more amazed. There were the four funnels, the lifeboats and the lifeboat davits, the bridge, the wheel, the propellers, and the anchors. Blue paper water broke against the hull with white tempera foam. With his grandson deftly pointing out areas of interest on the model, Mr. Mason concluded his talk, and we went back to our classroom, inspired, awed, and educated.

This year, when the grandparents file in on Grandparents' Day, I run a practiced eye over them like an old judge at a swine show. Carl's grandmother, I happen to know, was born in Norway and is said to play the Hardanger fiddle. I catch her on the way out. "We will be doing a little unit on the Viking explorations next month," I say in my nicest voice. "I wonder if you would consider . . ."

Fireman for Life

I am a first-grade schoolteacher, a small-sized person, not very brave. I have no mechanical sense, loud noises make me jump, and I'm afraid of heights. Why, then, was my hand raised when they called for volunteer firemen down at the community center?

To establish a fire department, we had to have at least eleven volunteers; only ten hands were up. I was in the thrall of that good old rural community spirit. I'll be saving lives and property, I thought, raising my hand higher and higher. It was a noble gesture. Besides, I told myself later that night in a saner moment, surely, in a month or two, someone will come along and take my place.

Our training course lasted ten weeks. Every

Tuesday and Thursday night from six to ten o'clock
we were down at the agricenter tying slipless knots,
scrambling up and down ladders with heavy equip-
ment, and learning about toxic gases, types of fire
streams, and the laws of heat flow. We squirted great
holes and troughs in the sawdust of the stockyard
with a two-and-a-half-inch nozzle, and we spent a lot
of time crawling around blindfolded in the livestock
arena rescuing each other. I was everyone's favorite
victim. I'm easy to drag.

I had nightmares about "flashover"—instant and
complete conflagration—and being shut into hot,
tight, dark, smoky places. My replacement didn't
appear.

It came time to order our "turnout gear." It
didn't come in my size. The sleeves of the smallest
coat covered my hands. The smallest pants were so
big that I tripped over the cuffs as I climbed the
ladder. My suit had to be specially made. It took
three months. When I pulled it out of the box, it
looked like evening garb for one of Beatrix Potter's
rats. It fit perfectly.

There were contests to see who could get completely outfitted in under two minutes. I always
ended up three minutes late, with several female
snaps whose male counterparts could not be found,
and the red suspenders between my legs.

"But I don't want to be a fireman," I complained
to our chief. "I'm not good at it. I'm a schoolteacher.
Can't you find someone to take my place?"

"With what that suit cost the county," said our frugal chief, Lamar, "you're going to be a fireman for life—or until you can talk some little shrimp of a volunteer into taking over your gear." No shrimps showed up. It looked like I was going to be a fireman for a long time.

I started getting used to it. They elected me secretary, because of my neat first-grade-teacher printing, and they taught me how to work the pumper. I wait for the man at the end of the line to holler, "Charge it!" Then I flip three switches and make the gauge read 100 pounds before I open the valve. I also scrub the hose after every fire. Not very heroic.

The other day though, I got my chance. There was a wreck on 84, a head-on collision. Our jobs were to disconnect the batteries of both cars, wash any spilled gasoline off the road, direct traffic, and help the emergency medical technicians. I was at my station, ready to "charge it." But there was no spilled gas. Lamar was directing traffic.

A woman was lying in the grass beside the road. She looked dead to me, but the EMTs, who are finer judges of these things, were hovering over her, monitoring her diminishing vital signs and giving her little puffs of oxygen through a tube up her nose. One of the EMTs motioned me over.

"Her Bible. She wants her Bible. See if you can find it," he whispered earnestly.

The road was strewn with debris: broken glass,

papers, a rug, a dog leash, a Mickey Mouse hat—but no Bible. I rummaged through the wreckage frantically. I remembered the story of Stonewall Jackson, whose life had been saved when the Bible he carried over his heart deflected a Yankee bullet. Maybe this was life or death!

Finally, peering through a chink into the trunk of the car, I spotted it. The trunk was jammed shut. I got a crowbar from the fire truck and prized it open. But the book wasn't a Bible. Instead, it was a dog-eared, much-read copy of *Lady Chatterley's Lover.*

What was I to do? Should I tell the EMT there's no Bible? But she was so pale and so still. I had read about the enormous power of suggestion. The book had the heft and bulk of a Bible. I could just . . . But what if she died? The God some people believe in would send a person straight to hell if she died with *Lady Chatterley's Lover* in her hands.

Then something came over me. It felt like the same thing that had made me raise my hand in the community center. I took the book and placed it on her chest. I folded her hands on top of it. She hugged it and caressed the cover.

Within minutes the color rose to her cheeks, her eyes fluttered open, she snuffed a long drag of oxygen through the tube, moaned, and said, "Where am I? What's happening to me?" And as she gazed into the relieved face of the EMT, I deftly tweaked the book from her grasp and replaced it in the trunk of the car.

I may not be the biggest, bravest fireman in my county, but on that day, with a little help from D. H. Lawrence, I'm pretty sure I saved a life. It gave me a heady feeling.

Last week Lamar called me up. "There's a little man here. About your size. Wants to be a fireman. Want to let him try on your suit?"

"Nope," I said. "I'm a fireman for life."

The Dance of the Chicken Feet

When I was a little girl in first grade, our teacher used to make us play The Imagination Game. She would tell us to close our eyes. Then she would begin to describe something: a walk in the woods, a visit to a foreign country. "What do you see?" she would ask.

My classmates would call out, "Trees! Flowers! The Great Wall!"

Then the teacher would let us open our eyes. "This is the wonderful power of imagination," she would tell us. "With your imagination you can travel to faraway lands without ever leaving your home, you can see things no one else has ever seen, you can soar above the clouds!" Then she would tell us to close our eyes, and we would play The Imagination Game again.

The only problem was, I never saw anything—just black darkness. Sometimes I would peek at my classmates. There they would be, sitting on the rug with their grubby little fingers pressed against their squinched-shut eyes. I thought of the wonderful things they must be seeing: a swarm of tiny Chinese men all dressed in dusty black smocks and red embroidered slippers that turned up at the tips; a crocodile poking its eyes up through a duckweed scum; a little gap-toothed man with tiny red eyes peeking out from under a three-cornered hat and then disappearing into a deep hole in the ground. Why couldn't I see these things? I closed my eyes again. Blackness.

One day I confided in my teacher. "You know when we play The Imagination Game?" I said. "Well, I don't see anything."

"You don't see anything?" she asked.

"Just the dark," I said.

She called my mother in for a conference. "Your child doesn't seem to have any imagination," she told her. "Of course, she will learn to compensate in other ways. She can concentrate on math and the sciences. But I'm afraid it will be a terrible handicap to her in life."

My mother didn't seem too worried. But I was worried. I wanted to travel to faraway lands, see things no one else had ever seen, and soar above the clouds like my classmates. I practiced at home. I would sit in my room and play The Imagination Game. I would tell myself stories. Then I would squeeze my eyes tight shut. Nothing.

Finally there came a day when I did see something. Behind one eyelid I spotted a thin, squirming squiggle. When I rolled my eyes up, it would drift down. When I looked down, it scrolled up. "This is it!" I thought. "The germ of an imagination! If I can just concentrate hard enough, I can make it blossom into an Angus bull in a field of clover or a girl in a red dress picking a white flower from a saguaro cactus." But then I looked up too far, and the squiggle disappeared behind my cheek.

After a while I gave up. When they played The Imagination Game, I would just sit quietly with my eyes closed. Sometimes, just for the heck of it, I would call out something. "An eagle catching a fish!" I would say. "I see a boy milking a brown cow!"

The teacher would say, "Very good!" and I would squirm with guilt.

Then one day she told us a story about a mermaid. The mermaid was very beautiful, and sailors fell in love with her at first sight. I was sitting on the rug with my classmates, eyes closed. I had actually come to enjoy my peaceful, silky darkness. And then, with no warning, an image appeared. It drifted into my sight, focused itself, and glowed in the dark.

It was a pair of giant chicken feet. They stood there for a minute, toes turned slightly in; then they were gone. The next time we played The Imagination Game, the chicken feet appeared again. This time they moved. They did a little dance. One foot lifted up, toes dangling limply; then that foot set itself delicately down, and the other foot lifted up. From then on, whenever we played The Imagination Game, I would sit happily in my place and watch the dance of the chicken feet.

Years passed. I grew up and became a first-grade teacher myself. I almost forgot about The Imagination Game and the giant chicken feet.

Then last week an important children's book author visited our school. My students were very excited. They had read all her books and drawn portraits of her in oil pastels. At 8:30 everyone assembled in the auditorium for her presentation. She was very pretty, with lots of flashing jewelry and fringes on her clothes. She drew pictures on an easel; she showed us her newest book, still in manuscript form; she explained woodblock printing. I was impressed. My students were spellbound.

At the end of her demonstration, she folded her hands, leaned down to the children, and beamed at them. "Now," she said, "I want you to play a little game with me. Do you like to play games?"

"Oh no," I thought.

"Yes!" the children cried.

"It's called The Imagination Game," she said.

"Now close your eyes." She told them a story about a camping trip. "What do you see?" she asked.

Eyes squinched tighter shut. Little grubby fingers pressed harder. Finally someone said, "A tent?"

"A tent! Great!" said the famous children's book author. "What else?"

"A pond!"

"A campfire!"

"This is the wonderful power of the imagination," she told them. "It is your most important possession. You must never lose it." Then she said good-bye, and we went back to our classrooms.

I gathered my children together on the rug. I got everyone's attention. "Don't worry if you didn't really see anything," I told them. "If you just saw darkness, it doesn't mean you will have a hard, sad life." Most of the children didn't seem to know or care what I was talking about. But I imagined that a few of them looked relieved. I felt like I had done the right thing.

After school that afternoon one of my students came up to me. She seemed a little nervous.

"You know when we played The Imagination Game?" she said. "I did see something."

"You saw something?" I asked. "What did you see?"

"Chicken feet," she said. "Giant, dancing chicken feet."

Cultural Center

One Friday morning my first-grade class, another first-grade class, and two second-grade classes were packed into a bus, four to a seat, for a trip across town to the cultural center to see an exhibit of Indian photographs and artifacts. Only half of the group could see the exhibit at a time; the other half had to wait.

Our class was in the first group. The guide was an experienced teacher herself, a master of the explosive *shhh!*, with an eagle eye for the occasional exploring finger. "Don't touch," she warned. And she meant it.

The photographs were all in color, with a kind of orange haze to them, suggestive of glowing campfires and the sunsets of another time. The children all swarmed instantly to one huge picture depicting a chubby, half-dressed Indian man with a lickerish smile who was embracing an Indian woman with crimped hair stylishly slung over one shoulder. Her polyester buckskin dress barely contained her swelling bosom, and she was smiling out at the camera with a knowing look.

The guide wedged herself in between the children and the picture and read the caption: "Indians are very loving to one another. They never fight within their own clan." "Now, boys and girls," she digressed, deftly sneaking in a little vocabulary on them, "what's a clan?"

We proceeded to the next room. In the middle of the floor was a bearskin, small, about the size of a Shetland pony. The guide seated us around it, just out of reach. She talked about the importance of bears to the Indians. They ate them, they made clothes out of their skins, and they had a bear dance and a bear song. "Don't touch!" she snarled as one little yearning finger strayed across the carpet. I noticed a card in a plastic holder: "All skins courtesy of Hammond's Taxidermy."

On the wall were displayed a spear, a peace pipe, and a bow with arrows. All were decorated with white leghorn chicken feathers dyed red and blue. The guide explained the significance of each one in three sentences or less; then we sat around the ceremonial drum. The head looked like molded plastic to me, but she explained that it was real deerskin. "Don't touch. All week only one child has touched this drum," she said proudly, "and he was a fourth-grader."

We all gasped with amazement. "What happened to him?" asked one boy.

"He had to sit on the bus for the rest of the tour," said the guide.

"It's hot in the bus," said the boy.

"Yes," said the guide. No one touched the drum.

Then I noticed a man I knew—Mr. Fielding, the maintenance supervisor for our local hospital, a tall, dark man with a friendly face. He was peering at the pictures through his half glasses. He delicately fingered the chicken feathers on the peace pipe. "Don't touch," our guide snapped instantly.

I crept over to Mr. Fielding. I just happened to know that he was a full-blooded Cherokee Indian. "What do you think?" I asked.

"My heritage," he whispered.

"Shhh!" hissed the guide.

After a little Indian music from the tape player our tour was over. We had to wait an hour for the other group to see it. I seated my children on the front steps and read to them from a little book I'd picked up on Cherokee lore. I read the "Legend of the Rattlesnake." An Indian chief's wife had to be sacrificed because she killed a rattlesnake. But the rattlesnakes taught the Indians a song. If they sang it whenever anyone got bit, that person would recover.

"Now," I said, "a few years ago my aunt Belle got bit by a rattlesnake while she was picking up plums. I didn't know the Indian rattlesnake song. What do you think I did with her?"

One little boy raised his hand instantly and confidently. "Buried her," he said.

But I'm a professional. I didn't miss a beat. "No," I said, "I took her to the hospital as fast as I could, and the doctors there gave her medicine and she got well. That's how we do it nowadays. And all these things they've been telling you about Indians . . ."

But just then I saw Mr. Fielding heading for his car. I ran and grabbed him. I dragged him over to my class. "Look at this man," I said to them. "He is a full-blooded Cherokee Indian."

"Oooo," breathed the children.

"Look at his shiny shoes, his starched pants, his striped shirt, and his glasses."

Mr. Fielding squirmed. "Just stand there," I said. Then I explained and explained to my children about old times, modern times, bitter sorrow, deep regret, and the tragedy of loss. "Now you may go," I told Mr. Fielding.

Soon it was time to ride back to school. We were crammed into the bus and made it back just before lunch.

Later that day I saw Mr. Fielding. I apologized. "Teachers will do anything to make a point," I said.

He said he didn't really mind. "You're wrong about one thing though," he told me. "I do know the rattlesnake song. I sing it to myself every time some-one is brought to the emergency room with a snake-bite."

"Did you sing it for my aunt Belle?" I asked.

"Yes, I did," said Mr. Fielding.

"She got well," I said.

"Yes, she did," he said.

I'd never noticed the wise and ancient depth in Mr. Fielding's eyes behind the half glasses and the twinkle.

"And if you ever get snakebit, I'll sing it for you," he said with a smile.

Mortality

It really makes you feel your age when you get a letter from your insurance agent telling you that the car you bought, only slightly used, the year you got out of college, is now an antique. "Beginning with your next payment, your insurance premiums will reflect this change in classification," the letter said.

I went out and looked at the car. I thought back over the years. I could almost hear my uncle's disapproving voice. "You should never buy a used car," he had told me the day I brought it home. Ten years later I drove that used car to his funeral. I drove my sister, Louise, to the hospital in that car to have her first baby, and I drove to Atlanta in that car when the

192

baby graduated from Georgia Tech with a degree in physics.

"When are you going to get a new car?" my friends asked me.

"I don't need a new car," I said. "This car runs fine."

I changed the oil often, and I kept good tires on it. It always got me where I wanted to go. But the stuffing came out of the backseat and the springs poked through, and the dashboard disintegrated. At 300,000 miles the odometer quit turning, but I didn't really care to know how far I had driven.

A hole wore in the floor where my heel rested in front of the accelerator, and the insulation all peeled off the fire wall. "Old piece of junk," my friends whispered. The seat-belt catch wore out, and I tied on a huge bronze hook with a fireman's knot.

Big flashy cars would zoom past me. People would shake their fists out the windows. "Get that clunker off the road!" they would shout.

Then one day on my way to work, the car coughed, sputtered, and stopped. "This is it," I thought, and I gave it a pat. "It's been a good car."

I called the mechanic. "Tow it in," I said. "I'll have to decide what to do." After work I went over there. I was feeling very glum. The mechanic laughed at me. "It's not funny," I said. "I've had that car a long time."

"You know what's wrong with that car?" he said.

"That car was out of gas." So I slopped a gallon of gas in the tank and drove ten more years. The gas gauge never worked again after that day, but I got to where I could tell when the gas was low by the smell. I think it was the smell of the bottom of the tank.

There was also a little smell of brake fluid, a little smell of exhaust, a little smell of oil, and after all the years a little smell of me. Car smells. And sounds. The wonderful sound when the engine finally catches on a cold day, and an ominous *tick tick* in July when the radiator is working too hard. The windshield wipers said "Gracie Allen Gracie Allen Gracie Allen." I didn't like a lot of conversation in the car because I had to keep listening for a little skip that meant I needed to jump out and adjust the carburetor.

I kept a screwdriver close to hand—and a pint of brake fluid, and a new roter, just in case. "She's strange," my friends whispered. "And she drives so slow."

I don't know how fast I drove. The speedometer had quit working years ago. But when I would look down through the hole in the floor and see the pavement, a gray blur, whizzing by just inches away from my feet, and feel the tremendous heat of internal combustion pouring back through the fire wall into my lap, and hear each barely contained explosion just as a heart attack victim is able to hear his own heartbeat, it didn't feel like slow to me. A whiff of brake fluid would remind me just what a tiny thing I was relying on to stop myself from hurtling along the surface of the earth at an unnatural speed, and when I finally arrived at my destination, I would slump back, unfasten the seat belt hook with trembling hands, and stagger out. I would gather up my things and give the car a last look. "Thank you, sir," I would say. "We got here one more time."

But after I got that letter, I began thinking about getting a new car. I read the newspaper every night. Finally I found one that sounded good. It was the same make as my car, but almost new. "Call Steve," the ad said.

I went to see the car. It was parked in Steve's driveway. It was a fashionable wheat color. There was carpet on the floor, and the seats were covered with a soft, velvety-feeling stuff. It smelled like acrylic and vinyl and Steve. The instrument panel looked like what you would need to run a jet plane. I turned a knob. Mozart's Concerto for Flute and Harp poured out of four speakers. "But how can you listen to the engine with music playing?" I asked Steve.

I turned the key. The car started instantly. No desperate pleadings, no wild hopes, no exquisitely paired maneuvers with the accelerator and the choke. Just instant ignition. I turned off the radio. I could barely hear the engine running, a low, steady hum. I fastened my seat belt. Nothing but a click.

Steve got in the passenger seat, and we went for a test drive. We floated down the road. I couldn't hear a sound, but I decided it must be time to shift gears. I stomped around on the floor and grabbed Steve's knee before I remembered it had automatic transmission. "You mean you just put it in 'Drive' and drive?" I asked.

Steve scrunched himself way over against his door and clamped his knees together. He tested his seat belt. "Have you ever driven a car before?" he asked.

I bought it for two thousand dollars. I rolled all the windows up by mashing a button beside my elbow, set the air-conditioning on "Recirc," and listened to Vivaldi all the way home.

So now I have two cars. I call them my new car and my real car. Most of the time I drive my new car. But on some days I go out to the barn and get in my real car. I shoo the rats out of the backseat and crank it up. Even without daily practice my hands and feet know just what to do. My ears perk up, and I sniff the air. I add a little brake fluid, a little water. I sniff again. It'll need gas next week, and an oil change.

I back it out and we roll down the road. People stop and look. They smile. "Neat car!" they say.

When I pull into the parking lot, my friends shake their heads and chuckle. They amble into the building. They're already thinking about their day's work. But I take one last look at the car and think what an amazing thing it is, internal combustion. And how wonderful to be still alive!

One-Eared Intellectual

In my town there lives a man with an enormous intellect and only one ear. When I was a little girl, I thought that the two things were connected, that giving up one ear was simply the price you had to pay to be that smart. Later I learned that he had lost the ear in an automobile accident and had gotten his education in the usual way at Duke University.

Mr. Harris has a pair of glasses with an artificial ear attached to the temple. It matches his real ear perfectly; and as long as he keeps the glasses on, everything is fine. Around the house, though, and among friends, he doesn't wear the artificial ear.

I have an uncle who is very good friends with Mr. Harris. Every spring our families get together.

My uncle and his friend go out into the kitchen and cook and talk about Spinoza, and the rest of us sit on the porch trying to convince Mr. Harris's wife that those are not fairies living in her maidenhair fern, but rats. She's been making tiny furniture for them out of twigs. Being married for forty years to a one-eared intellectual has taken its toll.

Mr. Harris is not stingy with his knowledge. He loves to teach people things. His hobby is substitute teaching. So about once a month he calls me on the phone. "Any teachers sick or pregnant at your school?" he asks.

"No," I say. "We're all fine."

Mr. Harris's dream is that a teacher will take maternity leave. That would give him six weeks in the classroom, maybe more, if there are complications.

Mr. Harris could teach anything, but he always teaches physics. It doesn't matter if the class is supposed to be English, political science, history, kindergarten, or second grade—Mr. Harris just walks in, sweeps the teacher's lesson plans off the desk, and teaches physics.

Mr. Harris has been teaching physics as a substitute teacher for many years now, and the people in our town are remarkably knowledgeable in the subject. You can walk up to almost anybody on the street and ask, "Do you know any physics?" That person will get a wild look in his eye, gasp, and recite, "Yes, momentum is the product of the mass and the velocity of a particle." Or, "Hard radiation is ionizing radiation with a high degree of penetration." Or, "A watt is the power resulting from the dissipation of one joule of energy in one second."

You see, Mr. Harris is a vigorous teacher. He doesn't just wander around the classroom with a piece of chalk in his hand and mumble. He gets excited about physics. He yells. He bangs on the desk. He scribbles wildly on the chalkboard. And invariably, in his pedagogical heat, he will forget himself for an instant and whip off his glasses. The ear comes off too. It is an unforgettable moment. Whatever Mr. Harris is saying when that ear comes off is seared into memory forever. It's the ultimate audiovisual aid.

Christmas Party

Every December there's an article in every women's fashion magazine about the Christmas office party. The photographs show beautiful women eating tiny food and drinking wonderful-looking clear drinks that just can't be water, and wearing black velvet and swagging silk and high-heeled shoes and stockings with little glittering things on them.

Every man in the pictures is as handsome as the handsomest man you ever saw, and they're all gazing longingly through horn-rimmed glasses into the eyes of the sultry-looking women, whose split skirts fall open to reveal that the little glittering things go all the way up. There's a hint of mystery and intrigue, and the implication that under the spell of these wonderful clothes and the magic of midwinter, transformations will occur. Little niggling flirtations that have been going on all year will blossom, and ordinary people will be changed into the gorgeous creatures we see in the glossy pictures.

I have never been to a party like that. We do have a Christmas party at the school where I teach. We have it in the teacher workroom on the last day of school after the children have gone home. The food is all left over from the classroom Christmas parties—cupcakes with Santa Claus's face drawn on the top, little wreaths made out of Rice Krispies gummed up with melted marshmallows and dyed green with food coloring, and Hawaiian Punch at room temperature. Everyone silently avoids certain things: Those gingerbread boys came from Mrs. Robinson's class. Her room mother smokes in the kitchen, and there's always an ashtray flavor lurking behind the ginger and nutmeg.

We are all dressed for Christmas, certainly, but it's not the same as in the magazine. Mrs. Boatwright is wearing her Santa Claus pin, the one where you pull the string and his nose lights up, and Miss Meadows is wearing a sweatshirt she painted herself. She smeared one of Santa's boots, but she turned the smear into a reindeer. I always wear my red corduroy jumper on that last day, and red socks. No one tries the glittering stockings. The children would just pick all the glitter off at story time.

We all sit around the paper cutter in the broken

chairs that are stored in the teacher workroom and put our plates and cups where we can. The Secret Santas are revealed. I had drawn Mrs. Jones's name, and I had been secretly giving her little presents all month.

"I knew it was you," she says. "I recognized your writing."

"But I disguised my writing!" I wail.

"You disguised it that same way last year," she says.

I wasn't surprised to learn that Mrs. Sampson was the one who had given me the Rudolph the Red-Nosed Reindeer embroidered dish towel. I know her stitching.

Mr. Dale, the media specialist, is the only man at our Christmas party. For the past fifteen years I have had a little crush on Mr. Dale. There's something so comforting about the way he comes into our darkened classroom when I can't get the movie projector to work. He flips open a little door that I didn't even know was there on the side of the machine, reaches inside, clicks little levers, and snaps things into place. Then suddenly the big reels begin to turn, we hear "Dixie," there's the seal of the State of Georgia on the screen, and the movie begins. "There you are," says Mr. Dale reassuringly, and then he's gone.

But poor old Mr. Dale is so tired from reshelving books all day and running around with new filmstrip projector bulbs, and I'm a little dizzy from the effort of keeping my class under control this week, when they've got more red dye than blood in their veins.

After a while Miss Meadows spills Hawaiian Punch down the front of her sweatshirt, and Mrs. Boatwright's Santa Claus nose won't stop blinking. Even Mr. Dale can't make it stop. "Somebody pulled the string too hard," he says.

Finally we say "Good-bye, and have a Merry Christmas" to each other, gather up our things, and go home. I hang my Rudolph dish towel on the rack in the kitchen and put my feet up. Somebody pulled the elastic out of my socks at story time, and they are drooping around my ankles. I imagine Mr. Dale at home lying flat on his back with an ice pack on his head. Every time I close my eyes, I see Santa Claus's nose blinking.

"Next year," I tell myself. "Next year I'll get those glittery stockings."

Maine

Of all the fifty states, my favorite is Maine. I've never been there, but I've spent hours looking at it on the map. I love the way it sits, so still and silent, at the very top of the page. I imagine that only the finest people live in Maine. The extreme cold brings their best qualities to the surface, and the ones who can't take it just shrivel away or move south.

So every September, when the *Weekly Reader* sends my first-grade class our pen pal assignment, I pray that this will be the year for Maine. I have had class pen pals from Texas, Alabama, and California—all very good states in their way, but compared to Maine, well . . .

Then, finally it happened. I was teaching that

year in a tiny school in an unincorporated town in central Florida. The pen pal assignment came: "Ms. Brookshire's first-grade class, Blueberry School, Thornacre, capital *M* capital *A*." Maine! My wish had come true after all those years!

My class and I set to work. I taught them all about the fishing industry in Maine, lobster pots, and the rugged coast. I showed them pictures of deep pine forests, magical hayfields, and tiny rocky islands in the fog. It was hard work. It's not easy to explain rocks to a child who has only ever seen sand.

I told them about the incredible cold winters, and they drew pictures of snowy scenes. They kept coloring the snow yellow. "Snow is supposed to be white," I said.

"But we don't have a white crayon," they told me. It's not easy to explain snow to a child who has only ever seen water.

Potatoes are Maine's major agricultural crop, so we planted a row of potatoes outside our classroom. And we read every book by Barbara Cooney and Robert McCloskey. By the time I finished with them, those children knew more about Maine than the people who live there.

Then we began collecting mementoes from central Florida to send to our pen pals in Maine: Spanish moss, palmetto leaves, and things to eat—the heart of a palm with directions for cooking, and a whole sack of tiny, tart citrus fruits called kumquats (you eat the peel and all). Each child wrote a letter, and we sent pictures we had taken of our sandy, sun-stupefied little Florida town. I packed everything carefully into a box and wrote the address on the outside: "Ms. Brookshire's First Grade, Blueberry School, Thornacre,"—and I wrote it out, forming each letter with the loving precision of a veteran first-grade teacher—"M-A-I-N-E." I sent it priority mail, because of the perishability of the contents.

Then we waited. We waited and waited. Winter came. We wore long-sleeved shirts. The children got impatient.

"They're probably gathering up stuff to send us," I said reassuringly. "Rocks and white pine cones, maybe."

"And snow!" the children said. "They're gathering snow in a box to send us!" Then I had to explain all about snow again. From Maine, nothing but a cool white silence.

Spring arrived. Our potatoes bloomed. "They're probably collecting native wildflowers to send us, flowers with names and colors we've never heard of. Flowers from Maine. Maybe they've put the blossoms in a flower press and have to wait for them to dry," I told the children.

It got to be May. School was almost out. We dug our potatoes. We ate them boiled and fried. Then one day, during the last week of school, a manila envelope arrived. Inside were twenty-five identical letters, copied from the chalkboard. There was also a short note from Ms. Brookshire. "Dear Ms. White," she wrote through clenched teeth. "Thank you for your package from Florida, which has just arrived. I should tell you that MA is the abbreviation for Massachusetts, where we are located. The abbreviation for Maine is ME."

I imagined the kumquats, black and furry with mold, oozing slime. And my students' sweet and earnest letters, soaked with the drool from the rotting heart of palm. I never wrote to Ms. Brookshire, but I thought about what I might have said. "Dear Ms. Brookshire: I should not have to tell you that FL is the abbreviation for Fool."

Used Cars

"You're looking at right around three for a rebuild," he tells me. "Six for a new engine."

"Three thousand dollars?" I ask.

"It'll run you six hundred just to get the head off."

"But I only paid two thousand dollars for the whole car."

He wipes his hands on a greasy rag and shakes his head. "Tough luck," he says.

So that's why I'm standing in a Honda showroom talking to a salesman named Harvey with almost no lips and very white teeth. "I want to buy a used car,"

I say. "A good used car with not many miles traveled."

"Lucky you came in today, Bailey," says Harvey. "Have I got the deal for you. This here is your '91 EX wagon, top of the line. A previously owned car. Loaded, with only five thousand highway miles on it." He sweeps open the door of a low-slung black car. I stoop over and look inside. "We can give you a thirty-six/thirty-six warranty, no deductible, bumper to bumper."

I sit down in the car and hold on to the steering wheel. It's got a perforated black leather cover on it. The windshield is very clean. Harvey reaches inside the car and flips things up and down. "You've got your tilt, your cruise, driver's side air bag. Bailey, this was Mr. Pockman's own personal car."

"I don't know who that is," I say, "Mr. Pockman."

Harvey points to a flashing sign outside with three-foot-high letters: POCKMAN HONDA SALES.

"Oh," I say.

Harvey leans both hands on the roof of the car so I can't get out. "New price for this car is twenty four. Your price, Bailey, seventeen seven."

I close my eyes and put in the commas and the zeroes. "Let me out," I say.

"This is the best deal in town," says Harvey as he follows me to the showroom door. "This car will be gone tomorrow."

Toyota. This time the car salesman is a woman. I sigh with relief. I think, I can handle this. We sit down in an office the size of a rural mailbox. I make her explain everything: the thirty-six/thirty-six warranty, bumper to bumper, tilt, cruise, power train. I make her write the figures down.

Then we get in a little red Toyota, and she drives me down the road. She rolls up all the windows and lights a cigarette. She tells me that soon she's going to stop smoking by having acupuncture in the ears. They put needles in your ears and leave them there. "My baby sister quit smoking that way," she says. "But it's so sad she never got to enjoy the life of a nonsmoker, because she was killed in a car accident."

She checks the rearview mirror and changes lanes. "Now if she had been driving a Toyota, Bailey," she says to me cozily, "my baby sister would be alive today, because of the safety features."

All the blood drains to my feet. I feel weak. "Stop," I say. "Let me out of here."

After that, I'm feeling patriotic. Ford. The salesman, Cecil, is a tall, grandfatherly man. We look at cars in the parking lot. He shows me the Escort, the Taurus, and the Tempo. We talk about the features I would like to have: antilock brakes, air bag, heavy-duty suspension. I've learned some things. Tilt makes me nervous, cruise is spooky, and I get sick just thinking about a back-facing third rear seat.

"Tape deck?" Cecil asks.

"Yeah, I guess so. Sure."

Cecil nods sagely. "I suppose a teacher like yourself, Bailey, you like to listen to educational tapes. Now come into my office and we'll look at some figures."

Both the double doors are wide open, but Cecil puts his fingertips on my shoulder and gently nudges me toward the doorway, as if he believes that, left on my own, I might walk smack into the brick wall.

He sits behind his desk and adds up long columns of figures on a calculator. I perch on a chair by the wall and scribble on a pad I hold in my lap. I carry and borrow. "That seems like too much money," I say.

Cecil throws his ballpoint pen across his desk and rares back in his swivel chair. "Honey," he says, "you know what Robert E. Lee always said." Then he slowly leans forward across his desk and squints at me appraisingly. "You *do* know who Robert E. Lee was, don't you, Bailey?" he asks.

"Well," I squirm, "yes, but . . . what . . . "

"Robert E. Lee always said, 'It's the stingy man who pays the most in the end.' "

"Let me out of here," I say.

That night I have a dizzy spell. I feel a tingling in my ears and an uncontrollable urge to take up smoking. I try to listen to my favorite tape. It's Big Mama Thornton singing "Hound Dog." But I turn it off guiltily before she's finished. It's not exactly educational.

I go to bed. Every time I close my eyes, I see long

strings of zeroes parading behind snapping white teeth. When I go to sleep, I dream that Robert E. Lee pulls up beside me in traffic. He's driving a red Mustang convertible. "You *do* know who I am," he says to me, "Bailey, don't you?"

"Yes sir, I do," I tell him eagerly.

"I never said that about the stingy man," he says.

"I know you didn't," I say.

"Yet you just sat there," he says. "You didn't do anything. You didn't say anything." He gives me that long, sad look, full of resignation and regret. He shakes his head and pulls away into the traffic. From his tape player the Rolling Stones are singing "I Can't Get No Satisfaction."

The next day I go back to the Ford dealer. Cecil comes up to me.

"Let's go into your office," I say. I twitch away from his helpful fingertips and march right through the doorway all by myself. I rearrange the furniture. I shove everything over on his desk so I have room to write.

"Sit down," I say. I stand in front of him and look him in the eye. "Now," I say, "every time you name a figure, I want you to say all the digits. No smoking, no smiling, and no quotations from famous historical personages. Sit up straight. And don't call me Honey." I whip out my sheet of *Blue Book* prices. "I'll pay you eight thousand dollars for that car. You put new tires on it, and you give me a one-year unconditional guarantee. No deductible." He blanches and mumbles something. "Speak up, Cecil," I say. I sit down, and we go to work.

As I'm driving home in my new car, an old silver-gray Jaguar roadster slides up beside me at a stoplight. It's Robert E. Lee.

"What do you think?" I ask him. "I got it for six hundred dollars below average retail—a thousand dollars below their asking price."

Robert E. Lee doesn't say a word. But with a sweeping gesture he takes his hat off and bows his head to me. His silver hair gleams in the sunlight. He looks into my eyes, a long, peaceful gaze. Then the light turns green, and he's gone. I think, how wonderful to see a smile on that face after all these years.

Snake Show

"No out-of-town field trips," our administrators told us this year. Like schools everywhere, we are suffering from budget cuts. I was disappointed because it meant my class wouldn't get to go to the reptile show down in Tallahassee as part of our unit on snakes. So, one cold early spring Sunday afternoon I was more delighted than horrified when I found a big white oak snake living in my bluebird house. I poked him out with a stick, scooped him into a garbage can, crimped a hardware-cloth lid on top, and drove him to school on Monday morning.

It was warm in our classroom. The snake was lively. Every time I thought about reaching into the garbage can to grab him, he raised up at me and hunched his shoulders and looked me in the eye. The boa constrictor down at the reptile show never seemed that alert.

I stalled for time with a lesson on the reaction of cold-blooded animals to changes in temperature. The children were excited. They wanted to see the snake. The classroom grew warmer and warmer. Finally I had to tell the truth.

"The snake is so hot, I'm afraid to reach down in there," I admitted. "I'm scared he'll bite me."

"Put ice on him," someone suggested.

Well, we did. We got a bag of ice from the lunchroom. In five minutes that snake's whole personality changed. I reached down in the can and gathered him up. Everyone got to touch him and rub him the right way and the wrong way. They all learned about reptile scales.

But the next morning, when I went into my classroom at 7:30, the garbage can was empty. The snake was gone. As careful as I had been with my crimped hardware-cloth lid, he must have nudged it up with his nose and slithered out.

It's almost impossible to find a snake in a literature-based elementary school classroom. I scrambled through student portfolios and unfinished projects on the cut-and-make table. I shifted all the clay whales waiting to be fired and unstacked all the shoe-box swamp scenes. The bell would ring in five minutes. Then, there he was, in the reading center, crawling out of the Wildlife Treasury cards and heading behind the bookcase.

I hesitated only a second. He, being his Mr. Hyde self that warm spring morning, didn't hesitate even that long. He bit me on the hand, right between the thumb and the first finger. I shoved him back in the can, crimped the lid on tighter, and stanched the flow of blood with a wad of paper towels. By the time the children came in, I had composed myself enough to give a nice little lesson on the bites of poisonous and nonpoisonous snakes.

Later that afternoon we took the snake to some woods behind the schoolhouse and turned him loose. Every child learned the last and most important lesson of all as we watched him slide away and disappear into the leaves.

And that night, keeping my throbbing hand elevated while infection slowly set in, I read my students' writing and realized that they had learned more about snakes from my bumbling demonstrations than my classes in other years had ever learned from the smooth reptile demonstration in Tallahassee, with its rattlesnakes behind glass and its torpid boa.

In the end, I have to admit that these budget cuts may make better teachers out of us all. At least, that is, those of us who survive.

Jeanne d'Arc

I have in my possession an old children's book, the story of Joan of Arc, movingly written and wonderfully illustrated by a Frenchman named Boutet de Monvel. He has a way of using color and texture and a delicacy of line that makes you want to sink into his pictures.

I took the book to school one day to read to my first-graders. I had to change the French to English, but I tried to keep the high drama and charged emotion of de Monvel's old-fashioned, rhetorical style. I showed them the pictures: hazy summer days and misty moonshiny nights, the archangel Saint Michael glowing gold, and the costumes of the royal court, painted so that the children couldn't help reaching up to touch the page to feel the damasks and brocades of those robes.

The most glorious pictures are the battle scenes. There is Joan of Arc, leading the charge, with the head of her great horse bursting out of the frame and onto the next page, and the forward-thrusting lances, and the gleaming silver armor. And best of all, de Monvel has draped over Joan a filmy garment that billows out behind in the fury of the fray and unfurls itself in graceful tatters over the heads of her faithful soldiers.

The book was even more successful than I had thought it would be. Not a single child stirred, and when we got to those battle scenes, I could almost feel their eyes sucking the images off the page. At the end, I read de Monvel's personal note to the reader: "To be victorious, you must believe in victory. So remember, my children, this story of Joan of Arc, against the day when your country will call on you to give her all your courage."

Thirty pairs of hands reached out to take the book, and there was a chorus of voices, "Read it again!"

After school that day I looked through my Joan of Arc book before I packed it up to take home. I found some new smudges on top of the old smudges left on those pages by French children almost a hundred years ago. Then I thought of something. I turned to the title page and checked the copyright date. It was 1898.

Little French children six years old, reading that book when it was new, would have been just military age in 1914. And here am I, who should know better, in another century, with that very book in my hands, telling other children the same old lie:

> Dulce et decorum est
> Pro patria mori.

Micanopy

Every year or so I drive two hundred miles to a bookstore in Micanopy, Florida. I drive south, past the capitol and the government buildings of Tallahassee and on down through the middle of Florida. I drive through Mayo and Day, tiny little towns that are slowly being reclaimed by flora and fauna. Wisteria is quietly disassembling the abandoned Victorian hotel on the only street in Mayo, and spreading fingers of Bermuda grass grow out over the white streets of Day.

I drive past bogs where cypress trees encroach on the road and pitcher plants bloom in the soggy ditches. Barbed-wire fences have rusted through, and Brahman cows graze on the right-of-way. I drive for miles without seeing another car, and buzzards eating dead possums in the road barely lope out of the way as I approach.

When I get to Payne's Prairie, I'm almost there. I stop the car and walk around a bit. Payne's Prairie is a mysterious place, first described by William Bartram, an explorer and naturalist, in 1774, and little changed since that time. It is a fifteen-thousand-acre wetland, formed over millions of years as land gradually sank into underlying limestone caverns. The many sinks enlarged over the years until they all came together, forming the huge basin that is now Payne's Prairie. I can see for miles across acres and acres of wet prairie and marshland. Herons and egrets and sandhill cranes stalk through the pickerelweed and pennywort, and hawks wheel overhead.

There are just a couple of miles of solid ground on the far side of Payne's Prairie before you come to Micanopy. There's a sign that used to say Micanopy Ballpark before mildew obscured the lettering, and grass has grown over the lower stone sign that says Micanopy—Settled 1820.

There is only one paved street in the town, with buildings on only one side of that street. Big oak trees shade the storefronts, and their roots have humped up the sidewalk and crumbled the asphalt of the street. In the middle of the row of buildings is an abandoned municipal garage. It still has its brick walls with the arched openings of doorways and windows, but the roof is gone, and limbs of the oak trees hang over the walls and drop acorns into the Model A Ford roadster that is parked inside, rusting away under a rotten tarpaulin. The other buildings, once hardware stores and drugstores and feed stores, have given over to the peculiar and the exotic.

In one building a woman with a big face and generous features sells cameos and collects stray animals. Fans move the air down from the high tin ceiling, and from glass cases hundreds of sharp-nosed pink-and-white pinched faces peer up at you with one tiny bright eye, while from the grapevine jungle just behind the store you can barely hear the yelps and whines of the lost pets of Micanopy.

The next store, a narrow brick building with two tall windows in the front, sells bottles. Shelves have been fitted into the windows, and green, red, and blue bottles are neatly arranged to catch the sunlight.

Down by the garage another store sells used clothing. A purple velvet cape lined with black silk hangs outside the door, and inside you can buy anything from a pink rayon slip from the 1940s to hundred-year-old crotchless bloomers trimmed with lace and a flounce.

At the very end of the street there is a sturdy arbor covered with wisteria so thick that even at noon on a midsummer's day it is as cool and dark under that arbor as dusk in November. When people have had enough of the bottles and the bloomers and the winks of the cameos, they sit in the wisteria shade and drink lemonade or iced tea.

But the reason I drive the two hundred miles year after year is the bookstore. The building is tall, a beautiful pink brick. The sign says:

O. Brisky
Books
Old Used Rare
Bought and Sold
Out of Print Search Service

Even before you go inside, you can smell the old, used, and rare books. On sunny days Mr. Brisky arranges a collection of books on a table on the sidewalk. There are books in the windows and stacks of books on the floor just inside the entrance. From an open back door the misty green light of Micanopy shines into the dust. Tendrils of wisteria have crept in through the doorway and are stealthily making their way toward the religion and philosophy section.

Years ago, when I first came to Mr. Brisky's bookstore, I was so bewildered by the maze of shelves and the teetering stacks of unshelved books in the aisles that I had to ask for help. Mr. Brisky, sitting behind a stack of Bancroft's *History of the United States*, was reading. He looked up at me over his glasses. "Hearn," I said, "Lafcadio Hearn."

Mr. Brisky marked his place in his book and came out. He wound his way skillfully around and around the shelves and through the piles of books. His feet knew just where to step. I blundered along gently behind him. He plucked a book from a high shelf. With a deft swipe of the hand he rubbed the mildew off the spine and handed it to me: *Some Chinese Ghosts*, by Lafcadio Hearn. "Also this," he said, and handed me a beautiful Hearn book printed on rice paper in Japan with color illustrations. "Also three books about Hearn," he said, and tipped them out. He leafed thoughtfully through *The Life and Letters of Lafcadio Hearn*. "Nobody reads Hearn anymore," he said, and wound his way back to his chair.

After that day I learned to find my own way around. Mr. Brisky has labeled his shelves in his optimistic, slanting hand: Seafaring Books by the front window; Firearms, Hunting, and Railroads in the murky middle of the store; Disasters on a high shelf; Fiction against a bearing wall; War in a little cul-de-sac under the oscillating fan; and Religion and Philosophy heading out the back door, meeting the wisteria on its way in. Now I seldom have to ask for help.

When I first pull into town, I wander around for a while getting used to the green and the damp and the aggressive vegetation. I drink tea under the wisteria arbor, then I go to the bookstore.

Mr. Brisky looks up from his book at me over his glasses. "Nice to see you again," he says. I find all the books on my list, load them into the car, and drive out through the damp dusk of Micanopy, back through Payne's Prairie, and to the outskirts of Gainesville, where I check into a motel for the night. I read my books for a while and listen to water slurping in the air-conditioner.

When I go to sleep, I dream that all the people in Florida are gone, smothered by water hyacinths or poisoned by the bites of mosquitoes. I am slogging my way through Payne's Prairie, with only water and aquatic plants as far as I can see. The water is waist deep in some places, but I slop on and on.

When I reach dry land, I shove for miles through the tangle of grapevines and palmetto. I part a curtain of Spanish moss, and there is the deserted street of Micanopy. Huge oak trees are growing in the rumble seat of the Model A Ford roadster in the garage, and the toppled blue and green bottles glint and twinkle from their window between the leaves of a wisteria screen.

I stumble up to the bookstore through a jungle of ferns. Climbing hydrangea has gotten in at the windows and through the back door, and the Poetry section has sprouted a blanket of sphagnum moss. A mud snake lies in a pool under Firearms, Hunting, and Railroads, and an anhinga perches on a first-edition copy of *The Lore of the Train*, by C. Hamilton Ellis, and dries its wings. A sinkhole has opened up under Pirates and Treasure, and Ships and The Sea totters on the edge of it.

I step through the cattails and maiden cane into

the store. Mr. Brisky is in his place. I knew he would be. He looks up over his glasses. In the green light his eyes are as blue as the bottles in the window next door. I slosh toward him through a pond of duckweed and American lotus.

"Bartram," I say. "*Travels through Georgia and Florida*."

Mr. Brisky stands up. A two-toed amphiuma slithers under his chair. He makes his way skillfully through the pennywort. Lotus leaves sway on their long stems. Mr. Brisky knows just where to step. I swish along behind him. An alligator hisses at me from the Children's section. Mr. Brisky reaches up to a high shelf. A snowy egret delicately steps aside, and Mr. Brisky pulls down a book. With his old, practiced gesture he wipes the resurrection fern off the spine and puts the book in my hands: Bartram's *Travels*. Mr. Brisky smiles. "Nobody reads Bartram anymore," he says.

Finding Myself

People are always going out west to find themselves. In the seventies they went to California. Now they seem to be finding themselves in New Mexico. I have a cousin who found herself in Santa Fe a few years ago. She just wasn't happy in Georgia. Her parents worried about her. She couldn't get a job she liked. Then she went to Santa Fe and found herself in a crystal shop. Her mother went out there to see her and gave us the report. "Lou Ann has found herself," she told my mother on the phone. "She's so happy."

Then Lou Ann came home for a visit. She was driving a Jeep Cherokee filled with huge, wild-looking dogs (three-fourths wolf, Lou Ann said); at least a ton of beautiful multicolored rocks; dozens of crocus sacks full of strange-smelling herbs; and a big, slow-moving, silent man who was said to speak three dead languages fluently.

Lou Ann did seem happy—if placidity to the point of torpor can be called happiness. Her eyes saw things slowly, her once-nervous hands lay in her lap as still as cold lizards, and her frantically curly hair, which in her unhappy days had seemed to be yearning to leave her head to settle somewhere else for a life of its own, now lay on her shoulders as peaceful as drenched seaweed.

They came into the house trailing a wake of patchouli and sage and sat around eating macrobiotic rice while in the backyard the wolf-dogs neatly and systematically killed all our chickens. After a week they loaded the dogs and the rocks back into the Jeep Cherokee and drove off in a cloud of inner peace.

I once started out to find myself. It was 1970; I headed for California. But I never made it. The bus broke down in Fort Worth, Texas, and the driver told us not to leave our seats. The repairs could be made within an hour, he said. My seatmate was a hairdresser from Nogales and couldn't talk about anything but the hair of people I hoped never to meet. After four hours I just had to leave my seat. I walked the two miles back to the bus station and bought a ticket home.

Now this leaves me with a question: What about all the unfound selves wandering around the Western states? What happens if they are never claimed? Do they shuffle aimlessly about on the mesas and amble through the arroyos with that vacant gaze I saw in Lou Ann's eyes, hoping that every wild-eyed, unfulfilled visitor from the east will be their searching self? After many lonely, single-selfed years, do they begin to move more slowly and eventually turn into trees or rocks?

I don't know if these other selves read books, but just in case, I want to send a message to mine in California. Here it is: I'm not coming. I'm sorry. But I have a good job, I just put a new roof on the house, and completely on my own I have achieved that inner peace that only comes with middle age. Besides, I just can't face that bus trip. Go ahead and turn into a tree. Turn into a nice one—a coast redwood or a bristlecone pine. Lean away from the wind. And maybe in thirty years or so I'll take one of those group tours for retired teachers to the West Coast. I'll stand under you in my plaid Bermuda shorts with the elastic waist and give you a little pat on the trunk.